Mental Muscle: Managing with Purpose

By Jorie Saldanha

ISBN: 1522858547
ISBN-13: 978-1522858546

DEDICATION

To my husband who teaches me something new each day.

CONTENTS

1 Introduction 1

2 Strategic muscle 7

Definition 7

Workout Objectives 7

Getting buy-in from your team 7

Holding others accountable 7

Managing your emotions 7

Stretching 7

Warm Up 13

Managing your emotions 13

Getting buy-in from your team 16

Holding others accountable 19

Now, Workout! 23

Workout Log 24

Practice: Managing your emotions 24

Practice: Getting buy-in from your team 25

Practice: Holding others accountable 27

Cool Down 28

3 Transformative muscle 30

Definition 30

Workout Objectives 30

Managing through change 30
Demonstrating flexibility 30
Changing and wearing different "hats" 30
Stretching 30
Warm Up 35
Managing through change 35
Demonstrating flexibility 40
Changing and wearing different "hats" 49
Now, Workout! 52
Workout Log 53
Practice: Managing through change 53
Practice: Demonstrating flexibility 54
Practice: Changing and wearing different "hats" 57
Cool Down 58
4 Resolute muscle 60
Definition 60
Workout Objectives 60
Remaining consistent 60
Handling difficult conversations 60
Managing and providing feedback in the moment 60
Stretching 60

Warm Up 65
Remaining consistent 65
Handling difficult conversations 67
Managing and providing feedback in-the-moment 75
Now, Workout! 79
Workout Log 80
Practice: Remaining consistent 81
Practice: Handling difficult conversations 83
Practice: Managing and providing feedback in the moment 84
Cool Down 85
5 Organized muscle 87
Definition 87
Workout Objectives 87
Managing your time wisely 87
Setting goals 87
Planning ahead and being proactive 87
Stretching 87
Warm Up 92
Managing your time wisely 92
Setting goals 101
Planning ahead and being proactive 103

Now, Workout! 105
Workout Log 106
Practice: Managing your time wisely 106
Practice: Setting goals 108
Practice: Planning ahead and being proactive . 111
Cool Down 112
6 Nuturing muscle 114
Definition 114
Workout Objectives 114
Developing your employees 114
Understanding how to balance needs 114
Assessing and managing perception 114
Stretching 114
Warm Up 119
Developing your employees 119
Understanding how to balance needs 126
Assessing and managing perception 130
Now, Workout! 133
Workout Log 134
Practice: Developing your employees 134
Practice: Understanding how to balance needs 136
Practice: Assessing and managing perception . 137

Cool Down 138

7 Genuine muscle 140

Definition 140

Workout Objectives 140

Being transparent and credible 140

Demonstrating active listening 140

Providing balanced feedback 140

Stretching 140

Warm Up 146

Being transparent and credible 146

Demonstrating active listening 151

Providing balanced feedback 154

Now, Workout! 158

Workout Log 159

Practice: Being transparent and credible 159

Practice: Demonstrating active listening 160

Practice: Providing balanced feedback 161

Cool Down 162

8 Be STRONG 164

Definition 164

Workout Objectives 164

Putting all the muscles to work 164

Continually challenging your muscles 164

Sharing the knowledge forward........................164
Stretching 164
Warm Up 173
Putting all the muscles to work 173
Continually challenging your muscles..............179
Sharing the knowledge forward........................180
Now, Workout! 181
Workout Log 182
Practice: Putting all the muscles to work 182
Practice: Continually challenging your muscles 185
Practice: Sharing the knowledge forward.........186
Cool Down 187
9 What now? 188
10 Index...194
11 References 198

1 INTRODUCTION

I'm not going to lie. When I first became a manager, I had absolutely no idea what I was getting into. I'd been managed, and I'd seen my father be a manager for over thirty years, but that made everyone else qualified to do the job. I really didn't know what I was doing.

What I did know was how to lead people. I had grown my leadership skills throughout my entire life. Some people are natural-born, leaders as they say. This was something that I truly believe I was meant to do.

Now, looking back, after many years of managing and leading people, I can say there are some lessons that I would have loved to have learned right away. Of course, experience is what causes the best learning, but I'm hoping, that by sharing the lessons I've learned, you'll be able to be the most effective manager that you can be.

I can tell you no matter how experienced you get as a manager, there is always a new lesson around the corner. There's always something that will puzzle you, and make you feel as though you have no idea what you're doing or how you got there. Of course, that's the part I like most about being a manager. There are as many predictable moments as there are unpredictable ones.

Being an effective manager is hard work, and not everyone should be a manager. It's also thankless work. After all, most people blame their manager or boss for their shortcomings or why they got skipped over for the job or project they wanted. Those same people assume that their manager isn't working or that their manager could be doing more. Perhaps, that's true. I have met many managers who weren't effective, but I've also met many managers who pour their hearts and souls into their work, only for their employees to think they aren't trying hard enough. So, if you're an individual contributor working on your skillsets towards becoming a manager, cut your boss some slack. It's not always as easy as it looks, and you'll see that are you start to build up your own talents towards becoming one.

Don't get me wrong, managing is fun. I love it! But if you want to be continuously recognized for doing a good job, you need to pick something else to do for a living. To successfully achieve longevity in management, you need to find other ways to fuel yourself.

So what fuels me? If I've learned anything about managing people, it's that the rewards can be few and far between, but when they come, they are so worth it.

I remember the first time I coached an employee towards getting their dream job position. They had been in their role for years and were starting to get very, very frustrated. They said to me one day that they didn't know if they could do it anymore.

I said, "If you can't do it now, here, what makes

you think you'll be able to do it somewhere else?" They didn't have an answer for me then. It was in that moment that we really started focusing on their goals and what it was going to take to get to the job what they did want. If they were serious about moving on, we were going to get them prepared for that role.

Their last day reporting to me was a bittersweet one. I will always remember and cherish the moment when they came up to me and said, "Thank you for all of your help. If it wasn't for you, I never would have gotten this job, because this whole time I was blaming everyone else for why my life wasn't going where I wanted. But you convinced me that it was my choice and within my power to get there. And now, I'm there!"

It's moments like what happened that day that fuel me to move forward. Being an effective manager isn't about telling people what to do or how to do it…well, okay. It's a little bit about that…and bossing people around *can* be fun. But, to be an effective manager and a true leader, you have to focus on the greater good. You have to focus on your team.

I'm clearly not the first person to have written about how to be an effective manager. I've attended more than my share of management and leadership seminars. So, why read my book? Why not, just attend one of those fancy seminars and call it a day?

I'll be honest. I've loved attending the different seminars, and those are great resources and places to fuel yourself, but sometimes, they are just too darn complicated. I can tell you, sometimes they are too much. There are so many principles and rules that are associated with being a good manager. It can be very overwhelming, whether you have one direct report or fifty. Which rules should you use and when? What's the right thing to say? What's the wrong thing to say? How will you know what to do and when to do it?

Those seminars don't have the answers for you. And I'm here to tell you, that I have absolutely no answers for you either. I'm not joking. Your eyes are not deceiving you. There is no single right answer to any of those questions. It comes down to taking control and making decisions. The only wrong decision is the lack of making one. Throughout this book, you'll find your own path and your own way to be the most effective manager you can be. All managers are not the same, and they shouldn't be. Not only would that be utterly boring, but it would eventually end very, very poorly. We need to have different management styles and different people, since we are all at a base level, different.

I want you to read this book to see that managing people can be simple. I'm not saying it's easy, but I am saying that you can break it down, and take it one step at a time. I'll take the different lessons I've picked up along the way, and relate them to you in a combined and simplified structure.

Learning to be a great manager isn't much different from training for a 5K. Success in either effort comes down to making a plan, following a structure, and making it happen. Muscles don't become strong for a 5K unless you challenge them and work them out. Very similarly, developing your managerial style requires a level of mental muscle. And, you can't get your mental muscle strong, unless you work it out and challenge it each day.

I've found that there are six mental muscles that you have to train and grow in order to manage with purpose. Once, you've fortified these muscles, you will be STRONG.

S	Strategic
T	Transformative
R	Resolute
O	Organized
N	Nurturing
G	Genuine

STRONG Model

Each of these muscles, requires a different set of skills and a different type of attention. Over the next few chapters, we'll look into each muscle to better understand what it takes to truly work it out. And, just like any work out, there will be workout objectives, stretching, warm-ups, the workout,

workout log, and cool down with each mental muscle group.

Without further ado, let's get our mental sweat on!

2 STRATEGIC MUSCLE

Definition

Strategic - Carefully designed or planned to serve a particular purpose or advantage (Hobson, 2004).

Workout Objectives

To be an effective manager, you need to build your mental muscle and become strategic in your thinking, communication, and actions. You'll find you need this muscle to work in conjunction with many of the other muscles.

After this workout you'll be stronger at:

- Getting buy-in from your team
- Holding others accountable
- Managing your emotions

Stretching

Let's see how strategic you are right now with this short quiz.

1. You and your team currently work Monday through Friday from 8 a.m. to 5 p.m. You have just found out from your manager that you will now be open on nights and weekends

and the entire team is going to have to support these new hours, including you. Which of these messages do you share with your team?

a. Team, we are going to be open on nights and weekends effective next month. This isn't going to be any fun for me either. We're in this together. So, let's do what we can to suffer through together. I've made a new schedule for each of you to work that includes nights and weekends, and I'll send that out to all you by the end of the day so you can prepare for next month's changes.
b. Team, we are going to be open on nights and weekends effective next month. I know this is going to be quite a change for most of us, but if we all pitch in together, I really think we can make this work, and increase our business as well. This isn't going to be any fun for me either. So, let's do what we can to suffer through together. I'll work with each of you to set up new schedules right away.
c. Team, we are being asked to provide more service to our customers when they need us most. We're going to move to a new hours model to better support their needs as we've been seen a lot of missed business when we're closed. Due to that,

we're going to be open on nights and weekends effective next month. I know this is going to be quite a change for most of us, but if we all pitch in together, I really think we can make this work, and increase our business as well. I'm going to send around a sign-up sheet. Please pick the days and times of the week that you'd be able to support these new hours so we can do our best to accommodate your work/life balance.

2. You're in a meeting with one of your employees who has been under-performing recently. You're asking them to improve their performance and are seeking their ideas of ways that they can do that. Their response to your question is, "My performance is fine. The problem is that you do not give me direct feedback in the moment. If you were managing me better, we wouldn't be having this conversation." What is your response?
    a. You need to start listening to me and doing your job or you won't have a job much longer. We're here to talk about your performance, not mine. How are you going to turn this around?
    b. I'm sorry to hear that you feel that way. Is there something that I could

be doing differently that would help you?

c. I hear what you're saying. If I understand you correctly, you feel that your performance is suffering as a result of my not providing you timely feedback, and I'm sorry to hear that. What I can do is set up more frequent meetings for us so that you're receiving the feedback as immediately as possible. With that in mind, let's get back to your performance. I am providing you the feedback now that it needs to improve. You're not meeting expectations and that's a problem. What can you do to improve, and how can I help you accomplish that?

3. While delivering a review with your employee about how they are not meeting expectations, the employee becomes very hostile and accuses you of being the problem. They begin to list several instances and situations that they feel are why you are an inadequate manager. What response do you provide?

   a. I'm sorry to hear that you feel that way. That deeply hurts me. I can't believe you would say something so mean and horrible. You are very difficult to work with and the reason you're getting this review is because of that. Not because of me. This conversation is over.

b. I'm sorry to hear that you feel that way. I have to admit that I'm very upset to hear you say that, but I understand that you have your own opinion. I'm going to take some time to look into these items you've brought up, and I'll do what I can to handle them.
c. I'm sorry to hear that you feel that way. I've taken some notes of your thoughts so that I can look into these further. I will set up some additional time for us to meet so that I can provide you with an adequate response to your concerns. In the meantime, I would like to revisit the performance items that led to your review rating. Let's discuss that now, and we'll revisit the other items during our next meeting.

Based on the number of A's, B's, or C's, determine your score. (If you have one of each, please read Mostly B's as this most accurately applies to you).

Novice Strategist (mostly A's)

You have a little bit of work to do to strengthen your strategic muscle. Currently, you act now, and think later, which isn't the best way to handle a situation. You're letting your emotions handle the situation. You tend to commiserate with your team a bit more than necessary, which can sometimes negatively impact your team's morale. While reading this chapter, focus on finding ways to further enhance your strategist muscles.

Moderate Strategist (mostly B's)

You're doing a fairly good job of using your strategic muscle, but you could use some improvement. You know how to collaborate and share options with your team, but still need to focus on thinking big picture. You're doing a good job of not letting emotions take over, but still need to make sure that you adequately prepare yourself before responding to a situation. While reading this chapter, focus on finding ways to further enhance your strategist muscles.

Strong Strategist (mostly C's)

Congrats! You're very adept at using your strategist muscle. You know how to explain concepts to others in order to obtain buy-in, and communicate in a way that commiserates without losing control of your emotions. While reading this chapter, focus on finding ways to further enhance your strategist muscles.

Warm Up

Managing your emotions

As a manager, you do not have the luxury of showing your emotions or having an opinion about something in the moment, especially in front of your employees. Why? Because you are "the face" of the organization to your employees. People stay or leave companies usually as a direct result of whether or not they liked working with and for their manager. The attitudes that you display as the manager have a direct impact on those you manage. Your employees will formulate their own opinions based upon how you behave and act. This is why it's absolutely crucial to control your emotions.

Keeping your emotions in a "lock up" of sorts is imperative especially when you're speaking with your employees. There's nothing wrong with having your own opinion about things, and there's also nothing wrong with having a reaction or emotion when something emotionally impacts you. However, you cannot let those emotions be viewed by your employees.

Why? If you have an emotional response, you can potentially lose the respect of your employee or possibly lose your job. Reacting emotionally can lead to stronger consequences when you're a manager because your actions are interpreted as the actions of the organization you represent.

There are a few situations where you'll be faced with the difficult tasks of keeping your emotions out of it. One situation is if you're feeling as if you're under attack. For example, if you're having a conversation with one of your employees about their performance, and they decide that it's completely your fault or begin to blame you, this can get very emotional very fast.

The best way to handle any situation that is emotionally volatile, whether it is positively so or negatively so, you should follow the emotion lock up process.

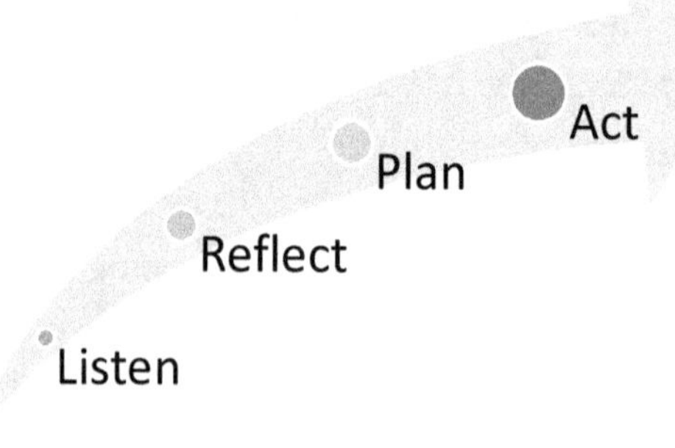

Emotion lock up process

First, you listen in the situation. This is the appropriate time to take stock of the situation. You listen and absorb all the information at hand. Keep your voice and facial expression neutral. One of the most important parts of listening is to not engage. Take a note of the information that is being shared with you, but do not provide responses in the moment, unless you feel prepared and able to keep your personal feelings out of the situation. Share with the employee that you want to listen and understand their feelings and will follow up with them to provide a response to what they have shared with you. This gives you time to have a response without feeling compelled to talk to the employee right away.

Once you've adequately listened, be sure to remove yourself from the situation. Go to a private place so that you can reflect on what took place. This is where you can have your own personal feelings or demonstrate your emotions. Make sure you do not have an audience for your emotional reaction.

Once you've had a chance to have your own response and determine your personal feelings, then it is time to plan how you will address the situation, if any response is warranted. You can also use this time to seek guidance from a peer or your manager to ensure that you are remaining factual rather than emotional in planning your response.

After the appropriate response has been determined, then you it is time for you to act on your plan and follow up as needed with all necessary parties.

By following this process, you ensure that you

keep your personal feelings to yourself and represent yourself as the face of the organization in a way that doesn't threaten your position or the respect of your employees.

Getting buy-in from your team

It's great to be able to demonstrate strategic actions, but being able to control your own actions and emotions is only part of the battle. The bigger difficulty lies in getting your team and those around you to also act the way that you need them to in order to foster the results you want.

Have you ever been in a meeting when a new process was rolled out and mostly everyone was excited for the updates? Well, everyone except for Bill, that *one* guy that just never likes anything changing or updating even if it will make his life easier. Have you had a "Bill" in your meeting? Bill is not unique. Many people are slow to buy-in to a new process. As the manager, it's your responsibility to get your team to buy-in to updates. This buy-in is very important as that's what leads to actual results. People perform better when they believe in or buy into a change, which means better outcomes and results in a business sense.

So, how do you get buy-in? Well, there are a lot of ways to do it. In fact, there are pages and pages of books about it. You can read all those books. I've read quite a few, but I have found there are two very simple steps to get people on board with anything, mostly.

Buy-in process

The first step, the "why," is a very important part of getting buy-in from your team. Everyone intrinsically wants to fight any change that happens, and the main reason is because they don't understand why the change has to happen in the first place. If you explain the rationale and the reason as to why something is changing, even if people don't agree with it, they are more apt to adopt the change.

The second step, the "options," is something I learned from a professional buy-in generator, my mother. Let me explain.

I was a young whippersnapper, willful to a fault, and unwilling to compromise…ever. Of course, I was a toddler, so "no" was my favorite word. At that age, I had decided that I would be very picky about my food. I didn't want to eat anything that was offered to me, even if it was food that I liked. Rather, I wanted to argue my way into eating whatever I felt was a better option at the time.

My mother quickly tired of this game of mine and decided to take action. It was time for dinner. I was fully prepared to say no to any and all food she gave me. My mom had other plans.

"Jorie, you have two options for dinner tonight. You can either sit down and have your peas or you can have your peas while you sit down. Which one would you like to do? The choice is yours."

Naturally, I was baffled at this. I had a choice? I was so excited that I held my head up high, and said, "Sit and eat." Very proud of myself, I sat down and ate.

Of course, the options my mother gave me were the exact same option no matter which one I picked, but I certainly didn't realize that. All I had really wanted was the ability to make a choice rather than just being told what to do.

The lesson here, is that we all want choices. Although we all like to think of ourselves as adults, we're really no different than that child version of myself, throwing a tantrum when we're told to do something and not being offered options.

Whenever there is a change or a new process in place, step back and look at it. Are there any elements on the change that could be handled in more than one way? Would changing it make any difference to the outcome? If you're able to find one thing, even if it's small, and turn it into a choice for your staff, do it. For example, "Would you all prefer to run this report before or after this caseload of work arrives?"

Something as simple as this has empowered my team to feel as though they had a choice and were part of the process rather than just a product of it. Overall did they get to change how the process worked? No. But, they did get to have a say in parts of the process, which made all the difference.

Holding others accountable

One of the more difficult aspects of being a manager is holding others accountable. This can be difficult no matter if the person you need to hold accountable is your manager, your peer, or your employee.

I know that whenever I need to have a very intense conversation with an employee, it can be nerve-wracking because the employee might not want to take ownership for their actions. This is why you must learn the manager mantra now and repeat it… often.

"I am a facilitator of events, not a perpetuator of events."

Manager mantra

Why is this mantra so important? Because it serves as a reminder to you of what your job actually is.

Let me clarify. You are responsible for calling attention to the actions of others and explicitly indicating to the employee whether or not it is acceptable behavior.

As the manager, you have to remember that you're not responsible. That's not to say that you don't have responsibility, but you're not responsible for the actions that someone else chose to demonstrate.

Many people find it difficult to share feedback or hold someone accountable to negative behavior saying, "I don't like confrontation." In reality, holding someone accountable isn't about confrontation, it's about calling attention to someone's actions whether they are or are not appropriate.

Think of it this way, would you ever be afraid to tell someone you were promoting them? No? Why is that? Probably because it's good news. Really, we're afraid to discuss difficult topics with others because the news might not be what the person wants to hear. Not only that, but we're afraid of the response that we might get. We think, "Will my employee blame me for what's happening?" or "Is there something that I could have done to avoid it?" We become very anxious about being called out by our employee.

So, when you're holding someone accountable, remember the mantra and that you're not responsible for their behavior, but you *are* responsible for telling someone if their behavior was or was not acceptable.

Typically, people who do not want to own their behaviors and actions will say something like, "Well, I'd be able to do XYZ better if you were a better manager." This is a flawed statement. Even if, you're not the most effective manager (though you'll be well on your way by the end of this book), it's not your fault that someone else made the decisions they did and took the actions they took. When someone says a statement like this, what they're doing is trying to call attention to your behavior and actions instead of taking responsibility for their own actions.

It's fair that perhaps you do have things you could improve in how you're managing, but your employee still needs to take ownership for their actions. I found an effective method of handling these types of distractions from the main point of the conversation and use the acronym ARCS to remember it.

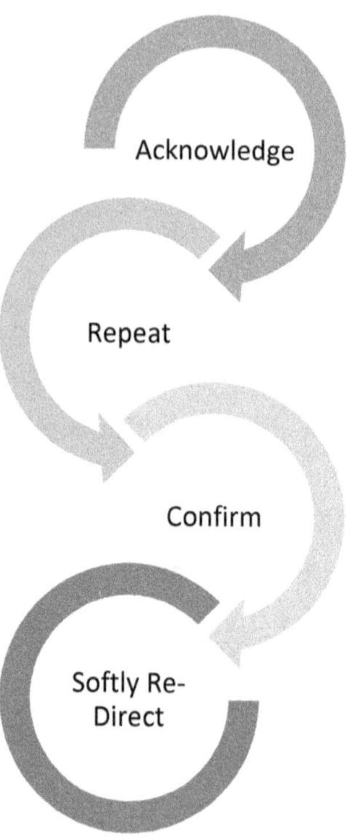

Arcs of a conversation

First and second you acknowledge what you've heard from the employee and repeat it back to demonstrate that you did in fact hear what they said and you understood them as well. Continuing the example above, "I understand that you're frustrated with how I'm managing. Are you saying that you feel I'm not managing you effectively?"

Once you've received assurance that you understood your employee correctly, you next should confirm what action you plan to take to address their concern by saying something like, "I can set up some additional time for us to talk later this week to address those concerns. If you'd like, please come with some examples so that I can start to address adapting my actions to better assist you."

Finally, you softly re-direct your employee back onto the original topic at hand by saying something like, "So, now let's get back to discussing the fact that you haven't been handling XYZ effectively. What do you plan to do to improve this?"

By executing the ARCS method, you'll be able to stay on point with your employee and make sure that they don't take control of the conversation and leave the conversation without understanding what they need to do to improve.

Now, Workout!

It's time to test out your strategic muscle by practicing what you've learned in real-life.

1. Identify a change that is taking place that you need to share with your manager, your peers, or your employees. With this change in mind, what's the why behind the change? What are some options that you can offer to your manager/peers/employees so they can participate more actively in the change?

2. In your next coaching conversation, test out the ARCS method to make sure that you stay on topic with your employee.
3. The next time that you are delivering "bad news" where you might want to respond emotionally, use the emotion lock up process and see if there's another way you can respond to the situation than how you previously would have.

Workout Log

It's helpful to map out your ideas and plan ahead. Use these practice sheets as your guide while exercising your strategic mental muscle.

<u>Practice: Managing your emotions</u>

Think of a time that you responded emotionally in a situation. How could you have handled it using the emotion lock up process?

What could you have done to listen?

____

____

____

____

____

What could you have done to reflect?

____

____

____

____

____

How could you have planned to respond?

____

____

____

____

____

What would your action have been?

____

____

____

____

____

<u>Practice: Getting buy-in from your team</u>

What is the change?

____

____

____

____

____

Why is the change happening?

____

____

____

____

____

What is a benefit of the change?

____

____

____

____

____

What options are there to handling the change?

____

____

____

____

____

What's the message that you want to share with your team with everything above considered?

____

____

____

____

____

Practice: Holding others accountable

Think of a time that you had an employee take you off topic by turning the conversation into a personal or professional attack. Write a statement for each letter of the ARCS method to handle the situation.

Acknowledge

____

____

____

____

____

Repeat

____

____

____

____

____

Confirm

____

____

____

____

____

Softly Re-direct

____

____

____

____

____

Cool Down

Now, you're equipped to be more strategic than ever!

It's important to use the emotion lock up process to prevent yourself from responding emotionally. This way you can respond factually and professionally without causing any undue harm to the relationship and respect you have with your employees or impact the status of your position within your organization.

Just as important as not responding emotionally, it's all important to provide your employees with the facts they need so they can respond appropriately as well.

Finding ways to share messages with others around you by thinking of the why and the options available will allow them to have a better understanding of the change as well as feel as if they are a part of the change. Doing this, will not guarantee buy-in, but it absolutely will improve the chances of adoption of any changes that have to happen.

Preparing yourself ahead of time and thinking of these things before communicating, will make you a more strategic communicator.

Although you may prepare yourself, sometimes, your employees will try to throw you a curveball. Whenever you're holding others accountable, remember that they might change to the offensive. Repeat the manager mantra to yourself and remember that you didn't cause the behaviors, you're simply holding your employee accountable to their behaviors. And, if your employee tries to change the subject, use the ARCS method to get back on track.

3 TRANSFORMATIVE MUSCLE

Definition

Transformative: Causing a major change to something or someone, especially in a way that makes it or them better (McIntosh, 2013).

Workout Objectives

To be an effective manager, you need to build your mental muscle and become transformative in how you approach your daily activities.

After this workout you'll be stronger at:

- Managing through change
- Demonstrating flexibility
- Changing and wearing different "hats"

Stretching

Let's see how transformative you are right now with this short quiz.

1. Your team is undergoing a massive change by changing databases for a system used most often to document interactions and business transactions with clients. You've just been

informed of the change, and are asked what to do to make the transition seamless. What do you do?

a. Read the documentation about the new software system, and share the information with your team the week before the launch, so everyone can get used to the new features.
b. Read the documentation about the new software system, and share the information with a few members of your team, as soon as possible. Have the team assemble a list of questions and suggestions for roll out. Share these suggestions with executive leadership, and implement them during the transition.
c. Read the documentation about the new software system, and share the information with a few members of your team, as soon as possible. Have the team assemble a list of questions and suggestions for roll out, and have them create a short training to provide to the rest of the team. Share these suggestions and trainings with executive leadership, and implement them during the transition.

2. You have been trying to have a meeting with your employee, Angela, for several weeks now

to complete a project that requires her skillsets. Each time the meeting is about to happen, she continually asks to reschedule the meeting. What do you do? The project deadline is coming up.

a. Find someone else that has similar skillsets to Angela, and ask that person to assist instead.
b. Go to Angela's desk or call her to determine why she continues to re-schedule. Ensure that she understands the importance of the project, and let her know you're adding another employee to the initiative to ensure it is completed on time.
c. Go to Angela's desk or call her to determine why she continues to re-schedule. Ensure that she understands the importance of the project, and let her know you're adding another employee to the initiative to ensure it is completed on time. Remind her that you will begin to remove her from projects if she's unable to make meetings or assist in hitting deadlines.

3. You are about to have a difficult conversation with Todd, who tends to blame others for work not completed. You are placing him on a formal warning to improve his performance or he could be terminated. You have prepared

yourself, and are ready to address any arguments he might have. When you sit down with him, he immediately shares with you that he's very emotional because a very close relative just passed away. What do you do?

a. Tell him that you're sorry for his loss. However, you do have something very important and time sensitive to discuss with him. Provide him with the formal warning.
b. Tell him you're sorry for his loss, and if there's anything that he needs from you, or if he needs to discuss anything. Once you've addressed those concerns, let him know that you have another important matter to discuss with him, but will set up additional time to discuss the following day.
c. Tell him you're sorry for his loss, and if there's anything that he needs from you to let you know. Also, if he needs to discuss anything to feel free to come to you. Once you've addressed those concerns, let him know that you have another important matter to discuss with him, and provide him with the formal warning, however express the information delicately, and less sternly than you originally intended. After discussing the

warning, let him know if he needs additional time due to today's events to absorb this information, that an additional discussion can be scheduled if he so desires.

Based on the number of A's, B's, or C's, determine your score. (If you have one of each, please read Mostly B's as this most accurately applies to you).

Novice Transformist (mostly A's)

You have a little bit of work to do to strengthen your transformative muscle. You're not currently very flexible with change and aren't always as adaptive as you could be when the situation warrants it. Take a look at this chapter and see what ways you can further enhance your transformative muscle!

Moderate Transformist (mostly B's)

You're doing a fairly good job of using your transformative muscle, but you could use some improvement. You're able to adapt to a situation, but still need to work on refining your ability to navigate change more smoothly. Take a look at this chapter and see what ways you can further enhance your transformative muscle!

Strong Strategist (mostly C's)

Congrats! You're very adept at using your transformative muscle. You're able to navigate change like a pro, and make sure to adapt your approach in a way that best fits the situation. Great job! Take a look at this chapter and see what ways you can further enhance your transformative muscle!

Warm Up

Managing through change

In many people's lives, the word "change" is a dirty word. It's something that many people fear and try to avoid if at all possible. Even if a change makes sense and would save money, time, and frustration, people will still fight it. Why is that?

I'm sure you can find many books and courses about that very topic, but I would assert, it all boils down to one central theme. The unknown. People fear what they do not know and do not understand, but the biggest personal growth I have ever experienced comes from stepping outside my comfort zone and into the unknown. That's where you really get to learn more about yourself and challenge yourself to be better.

Although, change is good for people, they still

fear it, because they don't know what to expect. As the manager, your employees look to you to understand what is expected and how to navigate change.

If that's the case, then how do you manage through change to make sure that things go smoothly? It's a three step process.

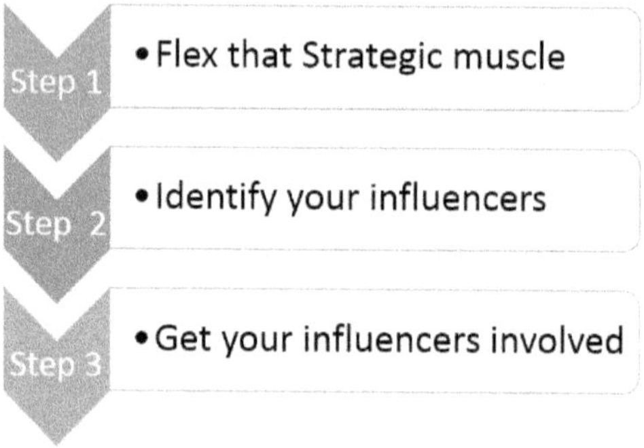

Step 1 • Flex that Strategic muscle

Step 2 • Identify your influencers

Step 3 • Get your influencers involved

Steps to managing through change

First off, don't forget to use your strategic muscle! Gaining buy-in is one of the central elements of making a change work. If you don't get buy-in from your employees, you might see change, but it will never be truly as successful as it could be.

With that in mind, make sure to explain the why and give your employees options. Get their buy-in. That's is one crucial part of managing through change.

The second crucial step to ensuring that change goes smoothly is to identify your influential employees. You'll want to find those individuals that are most open to change and get them involved as early on in the process as is possible. I call these employees Change Cheerleaders, and all Change Cheerleaders have some crucial characteristics that make them so vital to the change process.

Change Cheerleader

A Change Cheerleader, most importantly, is influential. What do I mean by influential? They are someone on the team that is deeply respected. They are the person that has the ability to impact the thinking of those around them. This is a very important attribute that you want to use to your advantage. If you're able to get the buy-in from the most influential person on your team, they will be able to encourage and lead the drive for buy-in amongst the rest of your team. After all, you want to work smarter, not harder.

In addition to having influence, the Change Cheerleader also, by nature, tends to be positive about most things, and is open-minded to how things will take place.

What if you have someone that is influential, but isn't actually positive or open-minded? This is definitely possible, and a much more dangerous type of person to have on the team as they are those employees that have influence, but are more negative and close-minded to change. These Adversarial Anchors tend to hold you back from getting change to take place as they expose negative thought processes to the rest of the employees.

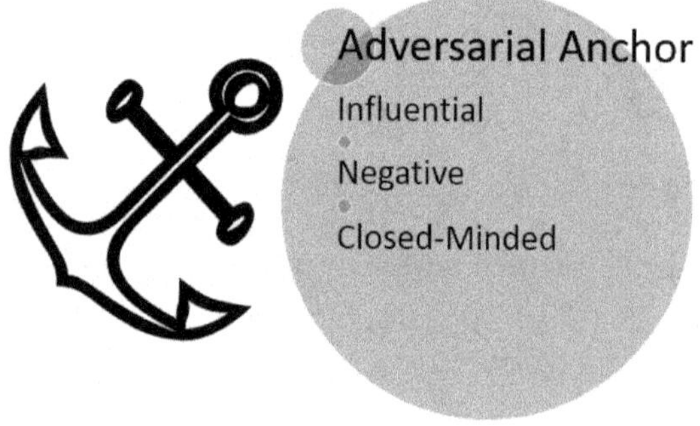

Adversarial Anchor

Now that you've identified your Change Cheerleaders and your Adversarial Anchors, what do you do? The third step is to get the influencers involved in the change. It's important that you utilize both of these types of influencers, as they are equally vital to the success of your change.

You want to get both the Change Cheerleaders and the Adversarial Anchors together and task them with assisting in facilitating the change. Ask them to participate in the change. Not only allow them the options and choices needed for buy-in, but also give them the chance to truly participate in the change in whatever capacity is possible.

Clearly, you want the Change Cheerleaders involved so they can better understand the change taking place and share that with your other employees so as to get buy-in faster. But…why would you want your least open-minded people involved in the change?

I'll tell you why! These employees are typically more resistant to change because they routinely feel excluded from the process or feel as if their opinions and viewpoints don't matter. When you put them front and center into a process with the ability to share their thoughts, they tend to be much less resistant. Also, there is a tangible benefit to having someone who is very critical of a process involved in change. They typically will spot flaws or areas of opportunity in a process long before anyone else will.

Be careful with your Adversarial Anchor though. You do not want to encourage negativity, but rather you want to encourage solution-based thinking. This is challenging a negative and problem-oriented person to not just find problems in a change, but also to propose potential solutions.

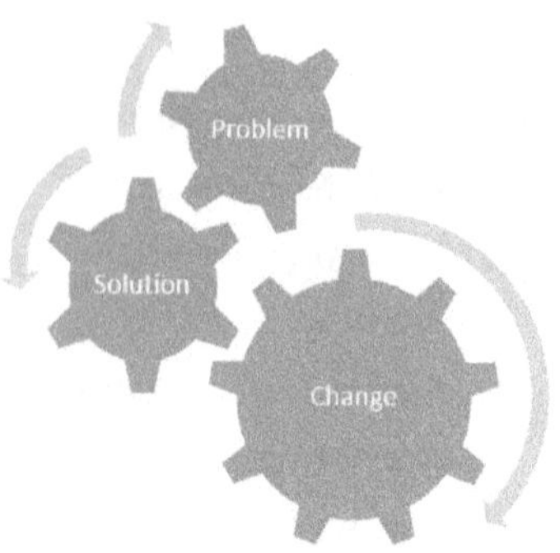

Solution-based thinking

By giving your most negative employees the chance to voice their concerns and the requirement to propose solutions, they are less likely to remain negative. I've found that when you task your most resistant and negative employees with providing solutions, they may sometimes opt to say nothing at all. They do this because they find it wasn't really a problem that needed fixing in the first place, thereby eradicating the risk of detracting and influencing others on the team from accepting a change.

Through the use of these three steps, you will find that change is adopted, and by involving others in the process, you're less burdened in owning all aspects of the change process.

<u>Demonstrating flexibility</u>

As a manager, it's important to be flexible to the needs of everyone around you, and this applies mainly to how you communicate. By adapting to what others need, you'll find that communication becomes clearer and simpler overall. There are three different elements that affect communication that you must alter and adapt as the situation requires.

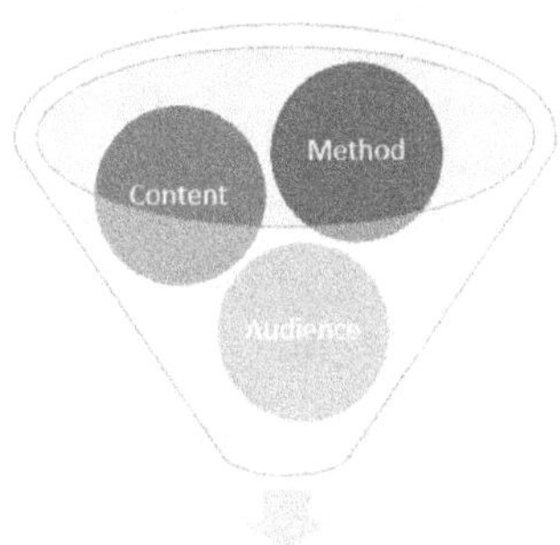

Communication

Communication elements

The first area that you need to understand and potentially be willing to alter and adapt is your communication method. What do I mean by this? Well, think about it. There are many different ways that you can choose to communicate a message to someone. You can choose to communicate with someone via face-to-face, video conference, email, instant message, social media messaging, texting, phone call, and many other ways that I'm sure are being invented as I write this.

Ultimately there are four larger groups to which each of these communication methods belong.

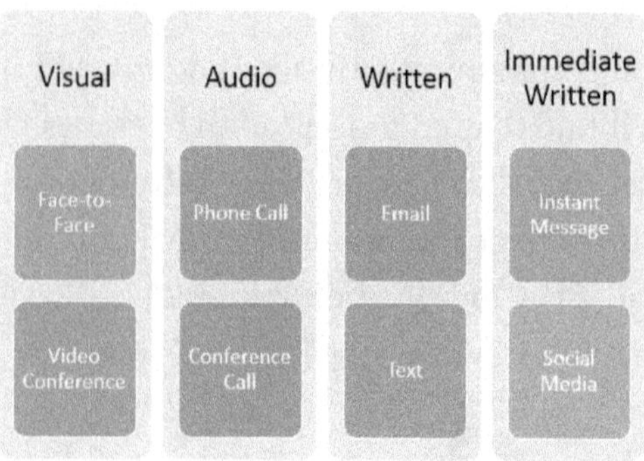

Communication methods

There are so many different methods to use to communicate to someone, but not all modes of communication are appropriate in all situations. All of these methods could potentially foster a different result, and each mode of communication has its own advantages and disadvantages.

Let me explain what I mean, by breaking it down by each communication method.

Visual communication is the original method of communication. You either shared a message face-to-face with someone, or you didn't share it with them at all. Almost all messages are appropriate to share using visual communication.

The advantage to visual communication is that both verbal and non-verbal cues can be understood by your employee. Your recipient will be able to see your facial expressions, hear your tone, and listen to your words to interpret your message.

Although visual methods of communication are usually preferable, a disadvantage is that sometimes it's not possible. As we move to a more remote and virtual environment, you may find that you're managing someone who lives in a completely different city, state, or country. It might not be feasible to have a face-to-face conversation with someone under those circumstances.

In addition to that, another potential disadvantage is that the visual method is literally in your face, and some people are uncomfortable with having some conversations this way. Some people may choose to use another method to avoid the more intense nature the visual method can cause.

The audio communication methods have the advantage of being less pressure as you're not able to see the person's face and they aren't able to see yours. Just as this is an advantage, this is also a disadvantage. Both you and your employee will need to use tone alone to truly interpret the non-verbal information being conveyed.

An advantage to using audio communication is that you're able to do this regardless of where the person you're speaking with is located. Especially with the wide utilization of cell phones, there really isn't a location that someone would be unreachable, in most situations.

A disadvantage of audio communication methods is that you're not going to be able to really know where the person is giving you their full attention or not. You can try to interpret if the person is giving you their undivided attention based off of their responses to your questions or the immediateness of their responses, but you won't be certain. Since you won't be able to see what else the person is doing this means there's the chance that your employee will not hear everything you're sharing with them and vice versa.

The written communication methods such as emailing and texting have a wider window for response. The advantage to this is that the other person doesn't need to be available at the time to receive your message.

Another advantage to written communication is that it is can be less awkward since the person isn't directly in front of you to respond to you. It also can be shared regardless of where you and your employee are located.

A disadvantage of using email or text to convey a message is that it is can easily be misinterpreted as word choice is the only way you can attempt to get your point across. Conveying tone and other nonverbal messaging is basically impossible, as the other person will most likely interpret any message you send based upon the mood they are in at the time of reading your correspondence.

Another disadvantage of written communication methods is that you cannot be sure that your message is received, viewed, and understood. Although you can put read receipts on some message or texts, you can't be sure that your message was fully understood, and you certainly can't guarantee a response the way a visual and audio communication method would.

The immediate written communication methods are more time sensitive. These messages are typically instant messages or are sent through social media and usually are sent to encourage an instant response compared to regular written communication, which unless explicitly stated within the message, doesn't have as tight an implied response expectation.

The advantages and disadvantages of written communication methods also applies to immediate written communication methods as well.

An advantage of the immediate communication method specifically, however, is that you can usually get more instant responses and move on with your day.

A disadvantage is that your message typically cannot be too complex as it usually leads to additional follow up or the need to use another type of communication if it is too complex.

Understanding these four different communications methods and their advantages/disadvantages is the first step in demonstrating flexibility in your communication. The second area to consider is the actual content of your message.

When you're communicating a message, you need to think about what the content of your message entails in regards to the complexity, time constraints, and nature of the message.

When it comes to the complexity of the message,

you want to consider a few things. Is this something that can be read and understood immediately or will follow up questions most likely occur? Knowing that the message may be more complicated may require that you use a specific communication method to make it more effective. You may choose to do a visual or audio communication method if the message content is complex so your employee has the ability to ask questions in the moment.

You'll also want to consider the time constraints of your message. Is there a specific timeframe that you need a response from your employee by or is it open-ended and not time bound? If you have a more immediate need you may want to choose visual, audio, or immediate written communication, whereas if you don't have a time constraint, the written communication method may be more appropriate.

Finally, you'll want to think about the nature of the message, meaning, is this a promotion or disciplinary message? Depending on the situation, perhaps visual or audio is most appropriate so that you're giving the employee time to share their thoughts and opinions with you in the moment.

By looking at the different aspects of the content of your message, you'll be able to determine the appropriate method of communication to use as well. However, you'll also want to take one more area of communication into consideration which is the audience. There are many elements to consider when looking at your audience which can be impacted by culture, generation, hierarchy, and personality.

When contemplating the audience for your message, consider that employee's culture. They may come from a heritage or country where certain methods of communication or content of communication are inappropriate. You do not want to stereotype and assume that you know what the person expects just because of the culture they are a part of, which is why you should ask your employee to make sure you understand any constraints or expectations.

For example, perhaps you have an employee who is Jewish and attends their religious services on Saturday. If would be inappropriate to request that the employee respond to you on Saturday, as they will be at their services at the time. However, you do not want to assume, just because the employee is Jewish that it's inappropriate. You would want to ask the employee first, which would also mean, you may need to use the visual or audio method to make this conversation simpler and more efficient.

You'll also want to take the employee's generation affiliation into account when communicating. Again, you do not want to stereotype and assume an employee's preference just because they are from a certain generation. However, if you have someone who was born in the 1940s-1960s, typically called Baby Boomers, they will most likely prefer visual communication over all other modes of communication and may even ignore all other forms of communication (Wall Street Journal, 2009). Understanding that may mean you need to adapt to their needs and communicate your message content using a visual method. Although, I won't delve into each generation and what they prefer and do not prefer, I highly recommend viewing literature on the topic as it is good reference information to assist you in making your communication method decisions.

Besides taking culture and generation into consideration, you will also want to think about the hierarchy of the person you're speaking with. If your employee is an entry level employee, you may want to alter the content of your message one way versus a tenured or senior level employee might respond better to a different version of message content.

Finally, you'll want to take the employee's personality into consideration. What do you know of their communication preferences? If you don't know, you should ask. There's nothing wrong with asking what someone's preferred method of communication is. This doesn't mean that you'll always be able to use that same method, but at least then you'll be aware of each individual's preferences.

As a last note regarding demonstrating flexibility when communicating, remember to try your best to adapt your method and style of content based upon the needs of your employees. Be willing to change from your preferred method of communication to cater to the needs of your employee. As the manager, think of your employee as your customer. You want to do your best to adjust to their needs. Although they may not appreciate the effort you take to do this consciously, they will certainly be more responsive to you.

Changing and wearing different "hats"

Another way you'll want to flex your transformative muscle, is in being able to adapt your approach and style to meet the needs of your team. Sometimes, you'll need to employ multiple styles during the same conversation to meet the needs of your employee. Each style, I consider putting on a different "hat." I'll go over each hat, and some scenarios when it would be necessary and appropriate to put it on. This isn't an exhaustive list, but it'll be a great start to your ability to transform and provide your employee with what they need when they need it.

I also want to mention that although a hat exists, you do not necessarily have to use it. Some people choose not to adapt and take on certain styles when communicating with their employees as a way to set more firm boundaries between manager and employee. This is completely your choice and is up to you. However, I've found that one of the best ways to elicit employee responsiveness, respect, and results is to use all the hats that I'll go over.

Hats diagram

The therapist hat is meant more for listening. This is a hat that some managers may choose not to use as they may feel it is more personal than they are willing to get with an employee, however I would say that this hat is necessary when your employee is facing a personal or emotional crisis.

You'll mostly want to listen and empathize. In the event that you feel the employee needs professional assistance, provide your employee with any of your organization's resources such as an employee assistance program.

The facilitator hat is used when you need to handle administrative situations such as paperwork or leading meetings. You'll want to be authoritative and remain on point. If people start to veer off topic, you'll be responsible for getting people back on topic.

The cheer squad hat is meant for providing

positive feedback and positive reinforcement to your team. You use this hat when you want to motivate and excite your team. You'll want to use this hat when sharing new programs, initiatives, and during team building exercises to get your employees in the right frame of mind.

The manager hat is when you have to pull rank and use your title or your place in the hierarchy to take control of the situation. You'll want to use this hat when hiring, promoting, disciplining, or terminating your employees. It's also appropriate to use this hat when you're instructing your employees of expectations or how to act.

The coach hat is meant to be used when you're assisting your employees with career growth and development. You use this hat to guide your employees in the direction that makes sense for that employee based upon the goals they have shared with you.

The mentor hat is meant to be used when you're either training new hires on skills that are needed to complete the job or when you're preparing an employee for a managerial role. The mentor hat is different from the coaching hat as you're setting more of an example and having a more hands-on approach, whereas the coaching hat is much more hands-off.

Try to think of which hats you'll need to use prior to a conversation with an employee. Also, while in the meeting, be adaptable and willing to switch into a different hat, if the situation calls for it.

For example, perhaps, you need to have a disciplinary meeting with one of your employees and have your manager hat on. However, before you can begin the conversation, your employee shares that a close family member just passed away. You should switch over to your therapist hat, and only move back to the manager hat once you've fully addressed all the concerns needed with the therapist hat.

By understanding these different hats and the appropriate situations to use them, you'll be able to better support your employees.

Now, Workout!

It's time to test out your transformative muscle by practicing what you've learned in real-life.

1. Identify a change that is taking place that you need to share with your manager, your peers, or your employees. How can you use your strategic muscle to gain buy-in? Who are the influencers? Which are Change Cheerleaders? Which are Adversarial Anchors? How can you involve them in the change so they can use solution-based thinking?
2. Think of an important message that you need to share with one of your employees. What is the appropriate contact method to use? Be sure to consider the content of the message in reference to complexity, time constraints, and

nature. Also, consider your audience. Are there any cultural, generational, hierarchy, or personality factors that impact the method and style of your message content?

3. Think of a difficult or intense conversation you've had with an employee. Which hats did you use in the conversation? Was it effective? Were there hats that you didn't use that you should have? How would that have changed the outcome of the conversation?

Workout Log

It's helpful to map out your ideas and plan ahead. Use these practice sheets as your guide while exercising your transformative mental muscle.

<u>Practice: Managing through change</u>

Think of change that is coming up. How could you have handled it using your transformative muscle?

What could you do to gain buy-in?

____

____

____

____

____

Who are the influencers on your team? Which ones are Change Cheerleaders? Which are Adversarial Anchors?

____

____

____

____

____

How could you involve your influencers in the change?

____

____

____

____

____

Practice: Demonstrating flexibility

Think of a message that you need to share with an employee. How will you communicate this to them?

What is the appropriate method of communication to use? What makes it the best method for this situation?

____

____

____

____

____

What is the content of the message?

____

____

____

____

____

Is it complex? Are there time constraints on it? What's the overall nature of the message?

____

____

____

____

____

Does this impact the communication method you're planning to use?

____

____

____

____

____

Are there any cultural, generational, hierarchy, or personality factors to consider?

____

____

____

____

____

Does this impact the communication method you're planning to use?

____

____

____

____

____

After going through this review, has your communication method or content changed?

____

____

____

____

Practice: Changing and wearing different "hats"

Think of an upcoming conversation that you need to have with one of your employees.

Which hats do you think you should use?

____

____

____

____

____

Why do you think these hats are appropriate?

____

____

____

____

____

Are there any hats that wouldn't be appropriate for this conversation? Why or Why not?

____

____

____

____

____

Are there any other topics that might come up where you would need to use a different hat? If so, what is the situation, and what hats would you need?

____

____

____

____

____

Cool Down

Now, you're equipped to be more transformative than ever!

You can transform and be able to manage through change by flexing your strategic muscle. It's important to explain the whys and provide options to your employees to obtain buy-in.

Although, you can obtain buy-in using your strategic muscle, you can also take it a step further by determining who your influencers are and which ones are Change Cheerleaders versus Adversarial Anchors.

By doing this, you'll be able to identify which key employees need to be involved in the change at the beginning stages so that you can get their buy-in and their influence to bring others onboard with the changes as well.

Being responsive to change is important, and being able to adapt your communication style is also imperative. You can demonstrate flexibility in your communication by carefully determining the appropriate method of your communication. You will be able to do this by weighing the factors of the content complexity, time constraints, and nature of your message as well as the culture, generation, hierarchy, and personality factors.

And, while you're considering the way you're communicating, you'll also want to always remember to wear the hat that best fits the situation. This way you can continually adapt to the needs of your employee by providing them with the assistance they need in the way they need it.

4 RESOLUTE MUSCLE

Definition

Resolute: Admirably purposeful, determined, and unwavering (McIntosh, 2013).

Workout Objectives

To be an effective manager, you need to build your mental muscle and become resolute in your decision-making and actions.

After this workout you'll be stronger at:

- Remaining consistent
- Handling difficult conversations
- Managing and providing feedback in the moment

Stretching

Let's see how resolute you are right now with this short quiz.

1. Two of your employees came to work late today. John is habitually having performance issues. This is the first time that Pam has had any inappropriate behavior of any kind. How do you address the behavior with John and Pam?

a. Pull John aside during the next 1on1 meeting and tell him if he's late one more time, he's going to be put on a formal warning. For Pam, you go up to her desk to see why she was late and then gently remind her the importance of arriving to work on time.
b. Discuss the attendance issue with both John and Pam during each upcoming 1on1 meeting and remind them that arriving on time is important and future occurrences could lead to disciplinary action.
c. During your next 1on1 meeting with John and Pam ask them why they were late. Depending on the reason, remind them that arriving on time is important and future occurrences could lead to disciplinary action.

2. You notice an employee being belligerent and rude with someone else on the team. This isn't the first time this person has behaved this way. They are a consistently difficult employee who routinely speaks to you with an immense lack of respect. The last conversation you had with them made you so frustrated and upset, that you took the following day off, just to get away from them.

What do you do when you see this employee exhibiting inappropriate behavior?

a. Set a meeting to talk with them in a week or so when they have cooled off and so you have enough time to really plan how you're going to talk to them. While in the meeting, ask them why they were behaving the way they were. Listen to their response and then let it go. It's been a few weeks, so it's not really an issue anymore.
b. Set a meeting to talk with them the next day to see what was going on with them and why they think this type of behavior was appropriate. While in the meeting, ask them why they are behaving the way they are. Listen to their response and remind them this behavior isn't appropriate, but don't push back too much once the employee insists that it wasn't their fault and to back off.
c. Ask the employee to meet you in a conference room right away. While in the meeting, ask them why they are behaving the way they are. Listen to their response and remind them this behavior isn't appropriate. When the employee is resistant to your feedback, remind them that the behavior cannot

continue. Offer to schedule some follow up time to discuss this further the following day when they can come to the meeting prepared and in a calmer state. As the issue warrants, schedule a discussion if additional items need to be fully addressed.

3. You see that Andrea is habitually not meeting her deadlines, and on this most recent project she not only didn't turn it in on time, she never turned it in. This was a high profile project with lots visibility to executive leadership. What do you do?
    a. Schedule a meeting with Andrea in a few weeks after you've resolved the issue as you're still trying to catch up on all of your tasks, and don't have the time to meet with Andrea now. Once you meet with her, explain the importance of deadlines and if she misses another deadline, she will be written up.
    b. Schedule a meeting with Andrea at the end of the week so that you have time to catch up on your other tasks. Once you meet with her, explain the importance of deadlines and if she misses another deadline, she will be written up.

c. Set a meeting with Andrea the same day that the deadline was missed. Once you meet with her, explain the importance of deadlines and if she misses another deadline, she will be written up.

Based on the number of A's, B's, or C's, determine your score. (If you have one of each, please read Mostly B's as this most accurately applies to you).

Novice in Resoluteness (mostly A's)

You have a little bit of work to do to strengthen your resolute muscle. You tend to shy away from difficult conversations, and aren't consistently providing feedback. You typically procrastinate to have the conversation, and by the time a discussion takes place, the information is no longer relevant. Use the next chapter to find ways to further enhance this muscle of yours!

Moderate in Resoluteness (mostly B's)

You're doing a fairly good job of using your resolute muscle, but you could use some improvement. You are comfortable having difficult conversations, and don't shy away from meeting with an employee in a more timely fashion. You still need to work on consistently enforcing your message, as you tend to back down when an employee objects. Use the next chapter to find ways to further enhance this muscle of yours!

Strong in Resoluteness (mostly C's)

Congrats! You're very adept at using your resolute muscle. You approach situations head-on, and don't wait for the situation to get worse. You are comfortable having difficult conversations, and are able to consistently enforce your message. Use the next chapter to find ways to further enhance this muscle of yours that is already quite strong!

Warm Up

Remaining consistent

There's an ongoing battle between treating everyone the same and handling every situation case-by-case. How can you do both? Is that even possible?

The answer is no. I know…you're all thinking I'm crazy at this point, if you haven't already been thinking that for a while. Here's the thing though, it's not possible to treat everyone the same, and you don't want to treat everyone the same because everyone's situation is going to be different. That's not to say that you should be handling all situations differently just so it's different. There are going to be lots of situations where you will handle things the exact same way.

The best way to remain consistent is to use a standardized approach that determines what action you should take. That's the key. By standardizing your process, you remove a lot of risk in treating people differently in an unfair way.

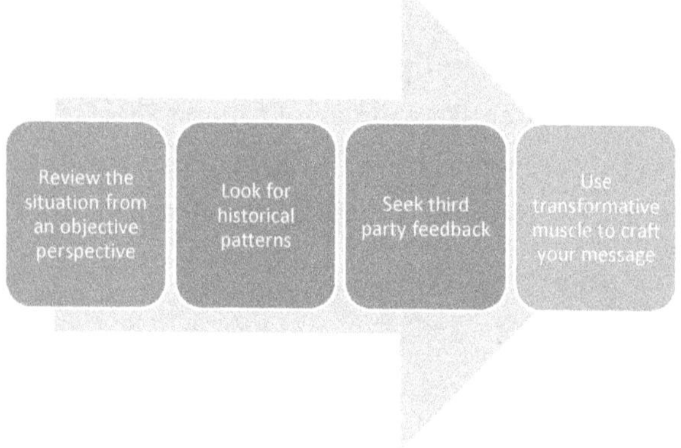

Standardized consistency approach

First, look at the situation objectively. Forget, for a little bit, who is involved and think about the facts rather than of the people. Handle the situation rather than the person. In order to do this, make a list of the behaviors that you have seen exhibited. Thinking from a factual perspective, historically have there been patterns with this behavior or activity in the past?

Based upon the facts of the situation, what is the expected or appropriate action you're required to take? Does this require a coaching conversation, formal documentation, serious corrective action?

After you've determined what you feel is the appropriate solution based upon the facts, seek out a third party such your peer or your manager. Provide them with the facts of the situation only. Do not provide the name of the individual. After you've shared the situation and your proposed solution, seek the opinion of your third party. Do they agree? Disagree? Should you change your approach considering their point of view?

Once you've determined what you feel is the correct next step, then it's time to use your transformative muscle and demonstrate flexibility! You'll want to think about your audience again and craft a message using the correct method and content that makes sense for that employee.

By following this method, you'll ensure that you are remaining consistent with all of your employees.

Handling difficult conversations

Now that you're aware of how to be consistent, it's time to actually approach what could be a very difficult conversation. For many people, one of the hardest parts about being a manager is having a difficult conversation with an employee. The fear that builds up before a difficult conversation can be intimidating and debilitating. It's all fine and good to know what you should do by being objective and consistent, but it's much harder to actually act on it, when you know you have a real live person you have to talk to about everything. The simple, hard truth is that you have to suck it up and deal with it. No matter how much you don't want to have the conversation, it doesn't change the fact that it's your job to do it anyway.

To make handling a difficult conversation easier, I recommend that you follow three steps. Following these steps will ease your mind, and make you feel much more confident when going into the situation.

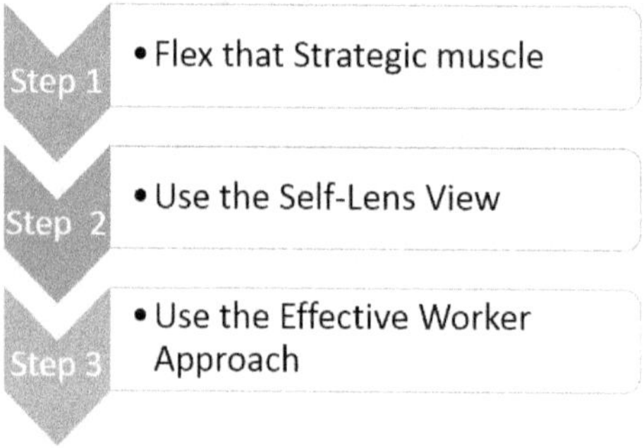

Step 1
- Flex that Strategic muscle

Step 2
- Use the Self-Lens View

Step 3
- Use the Effective Worker Approach

Steps to handling a difficult conversation

Your first step is to flex that strategic muscle! Repeat the manager mantra until you really internalize the words you're saying. You might have to say it *many* times before you really feel the power of the words. Don't stop repeating the mantra until you feel those words surging through your veins!

The second step, is to take the situation and look at it from a different view point. I call it the self-lens view. Let's work through this, as I know it's a slightly odd concept.

Think of the most irritating person who has ever reported to you. It's that person that continually argues with you, blames you when something goes wrong, blames others constantly, and overall, just seems like they almost *enjoy* going against everything you say. We've all worked with someone like that. If you haven't encountered someone like that, you are very lucky and should never complain ever again!

Seriously though, keep thinking of the person you have in mind while I tell you a time that I had to handle a situation with someone that was just like them.

I had someone who argued with me about every little concept. I'm pretty sure that even if they actually internally agreed with me, they would externally disagree and find a flaw in every single thing I did. They seemed to derive pleasure out of telling me all the ways that I was wrong. However, the bigger issue was that this person wasn't completing their work at a satisfactory level. In fact, they hadn't been doing so for a very long time.

I was going to have to sit them down to have a conversation with them about the fact that they needed to come up with some ways to change their behaviors and their work in order to remain at the organization.

I was not looking forward to this meeting, to say the least. In fact, I had been dreading this meeting, and I wanted to put it off as much as possible. However, I knew if I put it off, that it would still be an issue in the morning, so I resolved to meet with them as soon as possible. The problem I was facing prior to the meeting was finding a pleasant and professional way to share the message with them as they were so frustrating to work with.

After all, this person was not fun to be around and was very rude to me all the time. I was compelled to speak to them using the same tone they used with me. Yet, I knew that I couldn't actually do that. I was the manager. I had to take the higher road, not only because it's the right thing to do, but also because it was my responsibility as their manager to give them the information as clearly and factually as possible.

So, how did I prepare for this meeting? I needed two different methods to help myself make it through this meeting.

This is when the self-lens view comes into play. Turn the tables, and get back into the employee seat again. This requires that you think of what you would want to know and what would be important to you if the situation was reversed. What if you were the person with a performance issue?

Self-lens view

With that information in mind, now you know what you would need, but perhaps this employee is nothing like you. You know how you would want to hear it, but will that person respond well to the same approach? How do you make sure that you're staying objective, factual, and level-headed?

It's no simple feat, which is why it's now time to move to the third step of having a difficult conversation which is to use the effective worker approach. This is a method in which you prepare for the meeting, not thinking of this person, but rather thinking of how you would handle it with a different person. Stay with me on this.

If you were going to have the same conversation with one of your employees that had a great attitude and was very receptive to feedback, what would you say? How would you act? After listing out all the things you would say and do, how do they differ from what you want to say and do to your ineffective worker who is not receptive to feedback?

My guess is that the approaches are very different, and in a lot of ways, you don't want to say things the same way, however, you want to take a similar approach. The person you are speaking with shouldn't change the way that you speak to them or the message that you're wanting to get across. Altering your message that much means that you are probably editing it, which is something you do not want to do.

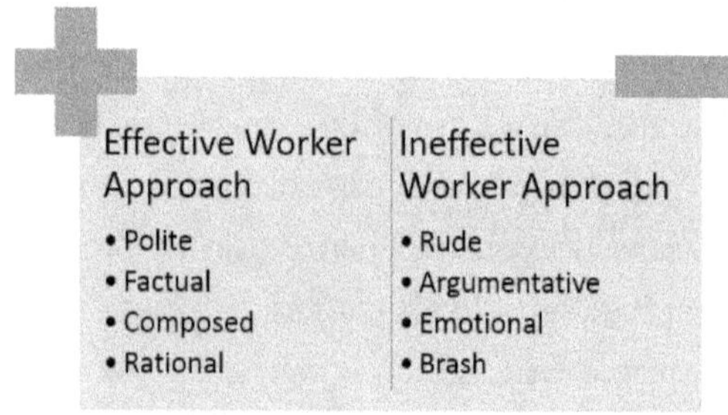

Effective worker approach

So, how did I do using these methods? Pretty good actually. I thought about an employee on my team who was receptive to feedback and thought about how I would tell them something if they weren't meeting expectations. What I discovered is that I would provide the feedback in an honest, but much less harsh manner. I decided to use this same method on my difficult employee. The results? Spectacular! The employee was extremely responsive to my kindness and professionalism. They even thanked me for giving me the feedback! I'd never had a response so pleasant over a difficult topic before, especially from this employee. Give it a shot, you'll see that even if you don't get a positive response from the employee, the method will work the way it's meant to work.

What do I mean by that? No matter what you say or do, the response your employee chooses to have to your conversation is completely up to them. Isn't that a freeing thought? Although it's important you share the message in the most professional and productive way possible, you are not responsible for the way your employee decides to act as a result of your conversation.

In fact, all employees will do one of two things in response to any coaching or disciplinary conversation you have with them. Yes, that's right. There are only two ways that your employee will respond. I call these two response the thrive or dive principle. This principle surrounds the idea that all employees will either improve their performance or they will continue to deteriorate in their performance based solely upon their own choice of how to respond to any instructions or feedback provided.

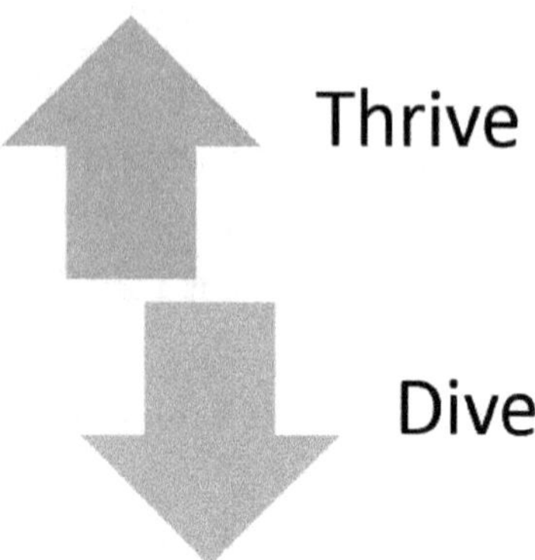

Thrive or dive principle

Whether your employee decides to thrive from your feedback or dive from your feedback is not up to you. However, it is your responsibility to continue to provide direct feedback and hold the employee accountable to whichever behaviors they choose to exhibit.

Meaning, if the employee decides to thrive with the direction provided, reward the behavior, and provide additional guidance to keep them on that path. If the employee decides to dive under the direction you provided, then hold them accountable and continually provide corrective action instruction until the employee eventually works themselves out of the organization either by resigning or being terminated.

Managing and providing feedback in-the-moment

It's great that you now know how to be consistent and how to navigate a difficult conversation, but those interactions require planning and careful consideration. What about providing feedback in the moment? How can you be sure that you're providing vital information to the employee when they need it?

At this point, I think a better question is, what's preventing you from giving in-the-moment feedback already? You'll probably find that you have a lot of different answers to this.

Many commons answers are that you're too busy, or you are too backlogged on other work, which is why you don't have time to give feedback in a timely way. If that's the case for you, you'll definitely want to work on strengthening your organized muscle, which is coming up next.

Some people struggle with giving timely positive feedback in the moment, and if you do, that's a simple and easy fix.

Are you ready to have your mind blown?

If you have something nice to say, say it! If you're taking the time to think about something good that your employee did, make sure that the next thing you do is actually share that information with your employee. Even if you do it through something as simple and as short as an email or instant message, that will go a long way with your employee.

However, I would argue that most people don't struggle with providing timely positive feedback, but more so on constructive feedback. I'm not talking about the intense conversations like disciplinary action or termination. Those conversations have a way of dictating that they happen timely either because the situation is getting out of hand or your manager is making sure you have the conversation.

I would say it's the smaller constructive feedback moments that lead up to those bigger conversations that managers struggle to give timely feedback about. I can't tell you how many times I've seen managers receive constructive feedback about their employee, but by the time they give their employee the feedback it is either out of date or has already been addressed by someone else. You don't want that to happen to you.

Why? If you aren't providing timely feedback, your employee will not view you as a strong resource or have faith in your abilities as their manager. If they are motivated, they will find others to give them feedback, leaving you behind. And, if they are a dishonest or low performing employee, they just might take advantage of the fact that you do not provide timely feedback. They could very easily take advantage of the "beg for forgiveness later" cliché.

You don't want this to happen to you either. So, how do you provide feedback in a timely manner on these smaller items? You'll want to use the in-the-moment feedback process.

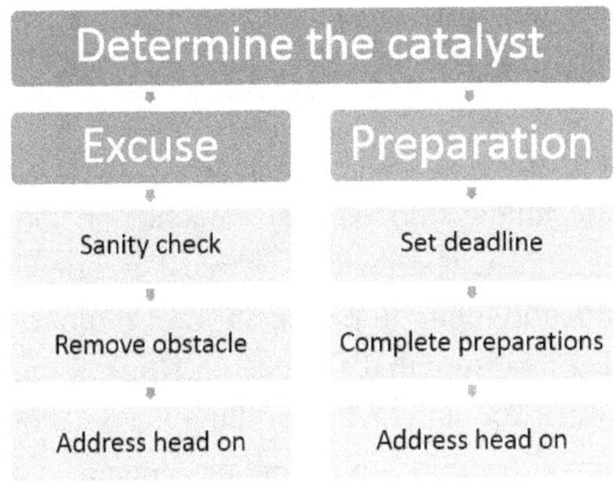

In-the-moment feedback process

You have to force yourself to give timely feedback first by determining what is the catalyst for not providing timely feedback. Is it fear? Are you anxious about the person's response? Do you need time to prepare?

Then it's time to determine whether the catalyst is an excuse or a true need for preparation. What's the difference? You'll know if it's a true need for preparation when you notice yourself going through the steps of handling a difficult conversation.

If that's the case, then you'll want to set a deadline for yourself of when you are required to be fully prepared and need to have the conversation with your employee. This way you ensure that you don't turn the need to prepare into an excuse to avoid a conversation. Once you've set your deadline, follow the steps necessary to prepare for your conversation. Once the deadline approaches, address the situation head on, and fortify yourself with the managing mantra, if necessary.

On the other hand, if your catalyst is an excuse, you need to follow a different approach. You'll know that it's an excuse when you know what you need to do in a situation, but you just don't want to do it. How will you be sure that's the case? Think about it very carefully. Would you be handling the issue head-on with someone who is pleasant and open to feedback? If your answer is yes, then you are just making excuses, my friend. You're looking to avoid a confrontation or conflict because it might be uncomfortable. You could also be crippled with fear.

It's time for a sanity check. What are you afraid of? Are you afraid of the response you might get? Don't let fear dictate your actions. Why would I say that? Remember the thrive or dive principle. It's not up to you how your employee responds, but it is up to you to ensure you provide feedback timely. If nothing else, provide the feedback to the employee timely so they don't have any accurate evidence to suggest you're not doing your job effectively.

You may just be anxious or fearful of the conversation because you can't control how your employee responds. You know that they will thrive or dive, but you're not able to control that, and that scares you. Everyone naturally fears what they can't control.

Do you know what I say to that? Control is an illusion. You have absolutely no control over anything or anyone. You aren't able to dictate anything except for your own actions. The only person or thing you are in control of is yourself. Other than that, you can't change anything. So, stop worrying about controlling the situation, because you've never had control to begin with!

So, now it's time to really acknowledge your excuses and remove that obstacle from the equation. Fortify yourself with the managing mantra if you need, but remember, you've already established that it's all excuses, so it's time to get to work. Address the situation, and you'll find that what you were afraid of typically doesn't happen and things tend to go much smoother than you could ever predict.

Now, Workout!

It's time to test out your resolute muscle by practicing what you've learned in real-life.

1. Identify a situation that you need to address, but want to be sure you're being fair. Review the situation from an objective standpoint. Are there any historical patterns? What action should you take? Does a third party agree with your assessment? Use the transformative muscle and craft a message with the

appropriate method and content for your audience.

2. Identify a difficult conversation that you need to have with one of your employees. Fortify yourself with the manager mantra and use the strategic muscle! Sit back and think of the situation from the self-lens view and the effective worker approach. Do you need to change your planned of action? Take action, but remember the thrive or dive principle.
3. Think of feedback that you need to give an employee that you may have been putting off. What's the catalyst for the delay? Is this an excuse or true preparation? Do you need a sanity check or to set a deadline? Remove all obstacles and address the situation head on.

Workout Log

It's helpful to map out your ideas and plan ahead. Use these practice sheets as your guide while exercising your resolute mental muscle.

Practice: Remaining consistent

Think of a conversation that you had in the past that you feel might not have been consistent with other similar actions you've taken. How could you have handled it using the standardized consistency approach?

What is the situation? Indicate it from an objective viewpoint.

____

____

____

____

____

Was there any historical pattern in this situation? What course of action did you choose to take?

____

____

____

____

____

Did you seek out the opinion of a third party? If yes, did they agree with your determined course of action? If no, how might that have altered your course of action?

____

____

____

____

____

Looking back on the situation, use your transformational muscle to craft a message using the appropriate method and content considering who your audience is. Was this different than what you actually said/did?

____

____

____

____

____

Would you have changed what you did with what you know now?

____

____

____

____

____

Practice: Handling difficult conversations

Think of a difficult conversation that you had in the past. How could you have handled it using the three step process?

How could the manager mantra have helped you?

____

____

____

____

____

What would you have thought of when using the self-lens view?

____

____

____

____

____

Think of an effective employee on your team, how would you have shared this message if it had been with them rather than your more difficult employee?

____

____

____

____

____

What do you think the result would have been if you'd used this three step approach?

____

____

____

____

____

<u>Practice: Managing and providing feedback in the moment</u>

Think of a conversation that you have been putting off with an employee. How could you use the in-the-moment feedback process to guide you?

What is the catalyst for avoiding the conversation?

____

____

____

____

____

Is this an excuse or the need for preparation?

____

____

____

____

____

If an excuse, write a sanity check reminder, and remove the obstacles preventing you from taking charge. If you need preparation, what's the deadline you need to set to have the conversation?

____

____

____

____

____

Have the conversation with your employee. How did the employee respond? Was it as bad as you thought it'd be or did it go better than anticipated?

____

____

____

____

____

Cool Down

Now, you're equipped to be more resolute than ever!

You can ensure you're remaining consistent by reviewing the situation from an objective point of view and looking for any historical patterns. By doing this, you'll be able to determine a course of action that you can run by a third party to get their advice and suggestions on the subject. And, you'll be more confident when using your transformational muscle to craft a message that has the appropriate method and content based on your audience.

By using the three step process of repeating the manager mantra, looking through the self-lens view, and thinking of the effective worker approach, you'll be able to change the way that you work with your employees. This changes the way you speak with them, which can lead to a whole new response and rapport with your employees.

Ultimately, you now know how to provide more timely feedback by looking at the catalyst for the delay, determining whether it's an excuse or a need for preparation. Then you'll be able to either force yourself to go through a sanity check or set a deadline for having the conversation with your employee. It's very important to remove any obstacles and complete your preparation, which will equip you to address the situation head-on. I know you'll find that in time, using these methods will make a huge difference in how your employees respond to you, and how you feel about yourself.

5 ORGANIZED MUSCLE

Definition

Organized: Having one's affairs in order so as to deal with them efficiently (McIntosh, 2013).

Workout Objectives

To be an effective manager, you need to build your mental muscle and become organized in everything you do.

After this workout you'll be stronger at:

- Managing your time wisely
- Setting goals
- Planning ahead and being proactive

Stretching

Let's see how organized you are right now with this short quiz.

1. You get in to work after a long vacation and your inbox is absolutely full with work to do. You're already feeling overwhelmed and you've only been back for ten minutes! How do you normally handle the situation?

a. Start at the bottom of the email list and work your way up. You might get a little side-tracked with other tasks along the way, but you'll eventually get through everything. You should be caught up by the end of the week, although you might miss a few deadlines before then if you haven't gotten to the email yet.
b. Look at your calendar to see what meetings are scheduled for the day to determine how much time you can dedicate to reviewing your email. Schedule time in your day to review email. When you are working through your email, start at the bottom of the email and work your way up. Typically, you'll be caught up within two to three days.
c. Look at your calendar to see what meetings are scheduled for the day to determine how much time you can dedicate to reviewing your email. Schedule time in your day to review email. When you are working through your email, start at the bottom of the email and work your way up. If the

item isn't urgent, continue onto the next email. Handle all time sensitive items first, then start back at the bottom to work the less urgent items. Typically, you'll be caught up by the end of the day.

2. You've been in your current role for several years and are looking for a new challenge, but aren't sure what that is. What do you do?
    a. Ask your manager for advice on what you should do, and based on what they say, start applying for new positions.
    b. Look up a few positions to see what types of new positions would be of interest to you. Make a list of the roles. Set up time with your manager to discuss stretch assignments or ways to develop your skillsets to prepare for the roles you've identified.
    c. Create a self-development plan. List out the current skillsets or activities that you do in your role that you enjoy, and then make a list of skillsets or activities that you do not do in your role and wish you did. Look up a few

positions to see what types of new positions would be of interest to you. Make a list of the roles. Set up time with your manager to discuss stretch assignments or ways to develop your skillsets to prepare for the roles you've identified.

3. You've just been told about an upcoming project that you'll need to get started on that will be due in a few months. It looks as though it will take about a week or so to prepare and complete this project. How do you approach the project?
    a. Begin the project a week or so before it's due so you'll meet the deadline on time.
    b. Set a reminder for yourself to begin reviewing the materials three weeks before the project is due, and then begin working on the project to give yourself a week of buffer if you hit any snags while working on the project to make sure you complete it on time.
    c. Review the project now, get a few ideas going and write them down so when you begin this project in earnest, you'll have a few ideas to

start from, but will also be able to review the project with fresh eyes in a few weeks. Set a reminder for yourself to begin reviewing the materials three weeks before the project is due, and then begin working on the project to give yourself a week of buffer if you hit any snags while working on the project to make sure you complete it on time.

Based on the number of A's, B's, or C's, determine your score. (If you have one of each, please read Mostly B's as this most accurately applies to you).

Novice Organization (mostly A's)

You have a little bit of work to do to strengthen your organized muscle. You tend to get side-tracked and stressed when there are many items that you need to complete or when you feel backlogged. You also need to work on finding ways to plan ahead and be proactive in your daily work as well as in your long term goals for career growth. Take a look at the rest of this chapter to see ways you can further enhance your organized mental muscle!

Moderate Organization (mostly B's)

You're doing a fairly good job of using your organized muscle, but you could use some improvement. You're able to plan ahead and get through a heavy workload without getting stressed. However, you still need to work on better developing your self-assessment skills in order to focus on your long term goals for career growth. Take a look at the rest of this chapter to see ways you can further enhance your organized mental muscle!

Strong Organization (mostly C's)

Congrats! You're very adept at using your organized muscle. You can handle heavy workloads like a champ. You're able to work in the day-to-day, prioritizing and setting both short and long term goals for yourself. Take a look at the rest of this chapter to see ways you can further enhance your organized mental muscle!

Warm Up

Managing your time wisely

Being able to manage your time wisely is essential to being an effective manager. Not only will disorganization prevent you from being able to use your other mental muscles effectively, it will also cause additional stress for you, which isn't good for your health or productivity. I know people say that they work well under pressure, and that may be true, but no one works well under the pressure of disorganization. The more stressed you are because you're "behind," the less productive you become.

I know the saying goes, "an apple a day keeps the doctor away," but I say a little COD is good for the bod!

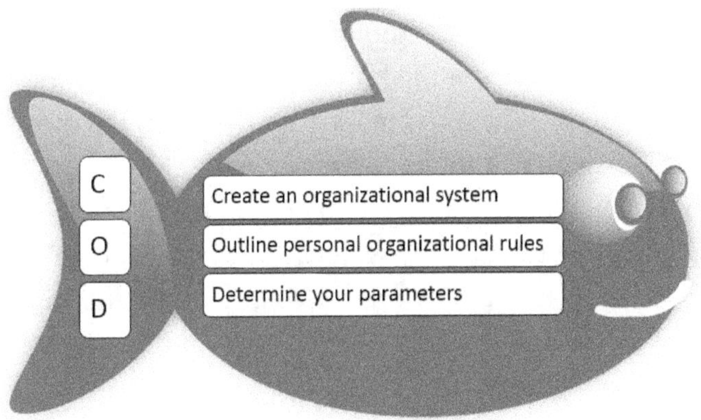

COD organizational approach

To ensure you manage your time wisely, you need to create an organizational system that is going to work for you, rather than against you. There are many different databases that you can pick from such as Outlook, Google, Excel, OneNote, etc. All of these programs have solid setups that will allow you to organize your day and keep track of what you need to accomplish.

Pick whatever system you want to use. I recommend that you use a calendar system such as Outlook or Google along with a document holding system such as OneNote or Excel.

The reason I recommend this is because you'll want to have a calendar that has your entire work day mapped out for you, but you'll also want to keep an ongoing checklist to keep track of everything you need to complete.

Your checklist should be continuously updated and ongoing. Make sure that you put any time sensitive items at the top of your list, and less important items at the bottom of your list. This way you can prioritize and work your way from the most important tasks to the last important tasks.

Whatever you decide to do, and whichever system you decide to use, pick something, and go with it. If it doesn't work for you, change it up, and switch to another method, until you find the system that works for you.

You can opt to have a physical calendar and checklist, a digital calendar and checklist, or a combination of the two. That is of little importance, but what is vital is that you have a system in place to track and manage your daily functions.

Make sure to schedule a few hours of time to initially setting up your organizational structure. I know that it sounds like a lot of time, but believe me, once you have it set up, maintenance of your system takes no time at all. You'll find that you'll be playing a lot less "catch-up" in you daily routine.

Once you've created your organizational system, it's time to outline your personal organizational rules. There are few rules that you can choose for yourself and a few rules I will recommend that you always use. I know that sounds super official, but I'll explain why you should do this and what I actually mean.

Within your organizational system, you need to establish how you want to store things. For example, will you create folders to store emails or use tabs to separate topics? The choice is yours, but you want to create a "rule" for yourself that dictates anytime you get XYZ email you please it in X tab or Y folder. By doing this, you discontinue the habit of staring at an email and vacillating on what to do with it.

You might not realize it now, but you spend a lot more time stewing with in-decision about how to organize something than you do actually organizing it. Once you've made the decision and rule of how you will use your folders, tabs, etc., stick with it. Use it, and if the rule stops working for you, change it so that it does.

In the calendar you keep, determine if you want to use color coding, and create rules for what each color represents. I would highly recommend color coding appointments and meetings, because when you look at your day, you'll be able to see what you need to do for the day, without feeling overwhelmed by a full calendar.

The way you assign the colors is completely up

to you and what makes sense to you. The idea is for you to create it so that it helps you be more efficient when reviewing your calendar.

For example, I use yellow to indicate that something is optional for me to do or attend. This way, if I see my calendar is full, but it's all full of yellow appointments, I know that my day is still clear, because I don't have to attend any of those meetings.

By establishing color rules, you'll provide yourself with a quicker guide to reviewing your calendar and knowing what you need to do for the day.

A rule that I recommend you set for yourself is making your email inbox your unofficial to do list. If you haven't addressed or answered it yet, leave it in your inbox. If you have already handled it, file it in a folder or delete it, depending on the situation.

By doing this, you'll ensure that you don't get overwhelmed by a sea of emails in an inbox and you also won't accidentally miss an important email among the other email clutter.

Next, determine what timing you want to use each day for checking email and updating your organizational system. You can choose to continuously update or set up recurring time each morning or each evening to update your organizational system. I recommend continuously updating your system.

What do I mean by this? Let's take an example. I continuously update and review my emails throughout the day. This way, I don't have emails back up and I never feel overwhelmed at any given time. However, you might find that tedious, so do what makes sense for you.

But, when you're catching up on emails either in the morning or when returning from being out of the office, work through them oldest email to newest email so you can understand the chronological nature of an email. As you work through your emails, read them and either handle them or move onto the next one. This is where the last rule I advise you set for yourself comes into play.

I call this the five minute rule. How does it work? The five minute rule dictates that if the email you're looking at is going to take longer than five minutes to address, move onto the next item until you've reviewed all your emails. Once you've reviewed everything, go back to the beginning and work through each email until you've completely cleared your inbox.

Something important to note, however, is that you should prioritize any time sensitive emails over others as well during this process.

Beware of one possible issue while using this practice that I like to call looping. This is when you continually read an email, decide it will take too long to address and move on. Be cautious of falling into the trap of looping. You end up wasting a lot more time reviewing and re-reviewing the email instead of just setting aside the necessary time to complete the task. Not only do you waste more time than it would have taken to complete it, but you also run the risk of accidentally missing a deadline.

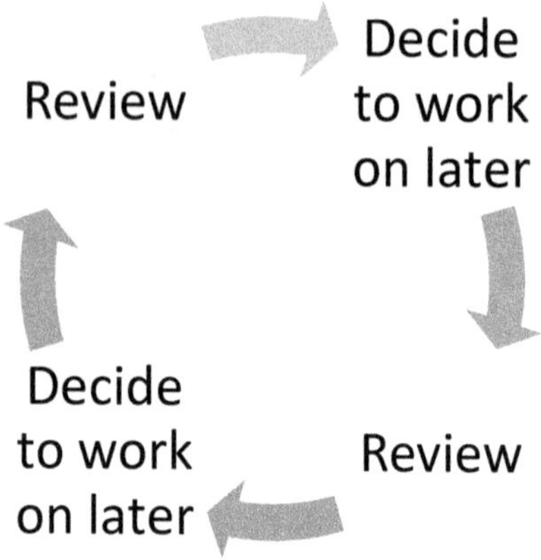

Looping

Once you've established both your organizational system and your personal rules, it's time to determine your parameters.

When I say parameters, I'm talking about understanding your personal limits and boundaries of what is and is not feasible for you. There is no one perfect or most correct way to stay organized. Everyone has a different method for staying on top of their tasks, but the results should always be the same. Meaning, your result should always be accomplishing what you need to on any given day.

One particular parameter to be aware of is your memory. Not everyone can remember a list of five or more items that need to be completed, which is why I recommend keeping a checklist. Know how much your memory is able to store, and try not to exceed that limit. Don't rely on your memory. Instead use the technology and resources available to notate and remind yourself of tasks that you might not remember to handle later.

Another personal parameter to be aware of is your ability to get distracted. Someone coming to your desk, calling you, texting you, etc. can distract you from getting your other tasks done. Determine whether you want to schedule time to review these habitual distractors or ensure that you're reviewing the "distraction" and then getting right back to the task at hand. However, I would definitely recommend scheduling time to review the habitual distractions as you might notice that you inadvertently spent your entire day on distractions rather than on work.

The last personal parameter that you want to be aware of is your ability to multitask. Let me be frank, I reject the expectation that everyone can multitask, because let me say, everyone cannot multitask. In fact, most people cannot, and fail trying, which leads to wasting time and being less productive overall. However, we all fall on a different part of what I call the multitasking spectrum.

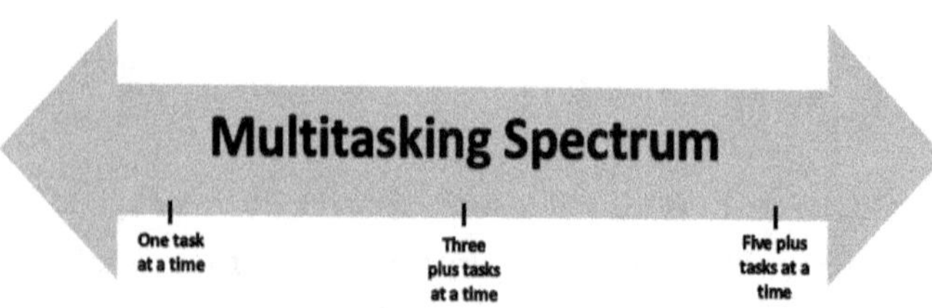

Multitasking spectrum

No matter what you do, you cannot change where you land on the multitasking spectrum. You can argue with me on that, but I've found that no matter how hard you try, you can't make yourself more of a multitasker than you are.

So, instead of trying to fight the type of multitasker that you are, embrace it! Understand what your limit is and make sure that you don't push yourself past that limit.

We all know when we've hit our multitasking limit. That's when someone says, "Hello, are you even listening to me?" or it's when we notice that we typed the same thing that we just said to someone when we meant to type something else entirely. These moments are when we're catching ourselves not functioning properly because we're trying to do too many things at once.

Instead of trying to do too many things at once, know your limit, and stick within it. You'll find that you're more productive and efficient this way. Why? Because you're wasting less time redoing work after failing to multitask, and accomplishing more…the first time!

By understanding this and all elements of the COD system, you'll be able to manage your time much more wisely and accomplish more.

Setting goals

Being organized isn't just about making sure you get all your tasks done when they are assigned. Yes, that's a large portion of it, but being able to set self-assess and set goals for yourself is just as important in order to be organized.

You want to take the time at least every six months to evaluate yourself and see what you're doing effectively and what you could be doing more effectively. This way you can update and revise your organizational set up to better fit your needs.

Not only do you want to be able to continuously improve your organizational skills, you also want to continuously improve yourself.

During this self-analysis you also will want to look into your immediate goals, short term goals and long term goals. Feel free to think of both the personal and the professional since they mutually impact each other. Your immediate goals are things you want to accomplish within the next day, week, or few months. Your short-term goals or things you want to accomplish in the next 6-12 months. Finally, your long-term goals would be things you want to accomplish in the next 2-5 years.

Create a self-development plan and ask yourself

these questions.

1. Short-term goals – what job and where do you want to be in the next 6-12 months? 1-2 years?
    a. What roles do you need to progress through to achieve your short-term goal?
    b. Which of these requirements do you currently possess and how can you further leverage those skills?
    c. Which of these requirements you not currently possess and how can you build those skills?
    d. What are the minimum requirements and skillsets of the role identified in the short-term goal?
2. Long-term goals - what job and where do you want to be in the next 2-5 years?
    a. What roles do you need to progress through to achieve your long-term goal?
    b. What are the minimum requirements and skillsets of the role identified in the long-term goal?
    c. Which of these requirements do you currently possess and how

can you further leverage those skills?

d. Which of these requirements do you not currently possess and how can you build those skills?

By identifying these different goals for yourself, you'll be able to set deadlines for yourself and review every few months to benchmark your progress. This will allow you to stay organized not only in how you manage your day, but also how you manage your personal and professional development.

<u>Planning ahead and being proactive</u>

Being able to plan ahead and be proactive sounds difficult, but is probably one of the easier things to do once you've perfected your approach to it, and much like other approaches, there are three steps to it.

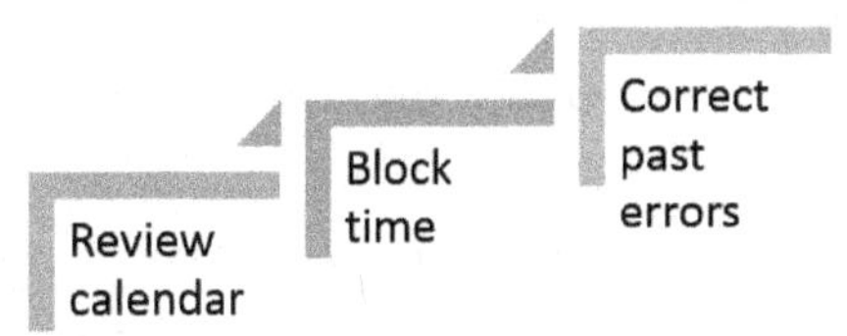

Proactive approach

Initially, you'll want to review your daily calendar. Look at your day in the morning, to get a sense of where the day is going to take you. Look ahead a few days and into the following week to make sure there aren't any larger projects or items that you'll need to complete.

Before you leave for the day, look at the following day to know what you'll need to be prepared for tomorrow.

You'll also want to block time on your calendar. What do I mean by this? Make appointments for yourself to work on specific projects or to prepare for specific meetings. This way you'll already have the time scheduled and it won't allow you to get side-tracked or forget.

Besides blocking time for work you need to complete, set up reminders for yourself several weeks in advance to revisit projects or initiatives that will take place in the future.

What do I mean by this? Let me give you an example. Let's say that I sent out an assignment to my employee and asked them to provide me with a proposal by the end of next week. Once I send that request out to my employee, I add an appointment on my calendar next week to remind my employee of the deadline. I also add an appointment on the day the project is due to remind myself to request the project from my employee. This forces me to be proactive, even if I'm not proactive in nature.

The last thing you'll want to do in order to remain proactive is to use your past errors and mistakes to serve you better in the future. If you missed a deadline because you only gave yourself a week to work on it last time, the next time a similar project comes up, give yourself twice that amount of time.

By using the proactive approach, you'll find that you're accomplishing tasks ahead of time and are less stressed because your organizational system is working for you, which will keep you calm while others are in crisis.

Now, Workout!

It's time to test out your organized muscle by practicing what you've learned in real-life.

1. Think of an area of your work that you wish you were more organized. What organizational structure should you use? What are some personal rules you should make for yourself with this structure? What are your parameters for this?
2. Create your self-development plan. What are your immediate, short, and long-term goals? What can you do to get where you want to go?
3. Think of an aspect of your job that you tend to procrastinate on. How can you review your calendar, block out time, and correct past mistakes in this area? Where are you on the multitasking spectrum and

how does this impact your way of handling your work?

Workout Log

It's helpful to map out your ideas and plan ahead. Use these practice sheets as your guide while exercising your organized mental muscle.

<u>Practice: Managing your time wisely</u>

Think of an area of your work where you would like to improve efficiency. How can you use the COD method to improve?

What is the organizational structure that you want to use for this area?

____

____

____

____

____

What are the organizational rules you need to set for yourself to remain efficient with your structure?

____

____

____

____

____

What are your personal parameters that you need to be aware of so you don't stretch yourself outside your abilities?

____

____

____

____

____

Where are you on the multitasking spectrum? How will knowing this help you avoid overextending yourself?

____

____

____

____

____

Practice: Setting goals

Think of your personal and professional goals. What do you want to accomplish in your life?

What job and where do you want to be in the next 6-12 months? 1-2 years?

____

____

____

____

____

What roles do you need to progress through to achieve your short-term goal?

____

____

____

____

____

Which of these requirements do you currently possess and how can you further leverage those skills?

____

____

____

____

____

Which of these requirements do you currently not possess and how can you further build those skills?

____

What are the minimum requirements and skillsets of the role identified in the short-term goal?

What job and where do you want to be in the next 2-5 years?

What roles do you need to progress through to achieve your long-term goal?

____
____
____
____
____

What are the minimum requirements and skillsets of the role identified in the long-term goal?

____
____
____
____
____

Which of these requirements do you currently possess and how can you further leverage those skills?

____
____
____
____
____

Which of these requirements do you not currently possess and how can you build those skills?

____

____

____

____

____

Practice: Planning ahead and being proactive

Think of an area of your work where you would like to be more proactive. How can you use the proactive approach to improve?

How can you review your calendar to keep yourself up to date in this area?

____

____

____

____

____

How can you block time and set reminders for yourself to stay on task?

____

____

____

____

____

What past mistakes have you made that you want to prevent? How can you prevent them from happening?

____

____

____

____

____

Cool Down

Now you, you're equipped to be more organized than ever!

You're able to use the COD method to create an organizational structure, outline personal organizational rules, and determine personal parameters. You can now understand where you are on the multitasking spectrum, and rather than trying to change it, you can leverage it and operate at your optimum efficiency. You've also learned that by prioritizing your workload, you're able to get through you work in half the time and avoid the trap of looping.

You're also able to organize yourself and self-assess by determining your strengths and your areas to improve, allowing you to set goals for yourself.

Make sure to take the time to think through your immediate, short, and long-term goals. Mapping out where you want to go in the future, will give you the motivation to remain organized and re-design your organizational setup if necessary to meet your changing needs.

Finally, you're able to plan ahead by using the proactive approach to review your calendar, block out time to complete items, and correct any past errors to prevent them from happening again in the future.

Continue to work on your organized muscle. By focusing on it, you'll see that your stress levels will plummet and your performance will skyrocket.

6 NUTURING MUSCLE

Definition

Nurturing: To help a plan or a person to develop and be successful (McIntosh, 2013).

Workout Objectives

To be an effective manager, you need to build your mental muscle and become nurturing to those around you.

After this workout you'll be stronger at:

- Developing your employees
- Understanding how to balance needs
- Assessing and managing perception

Stretching

Let's see how nurturing you are right now with this short quiz.

1. You're in a meeting with one of your employees who is very motivated to be promoted and move up in the company. They ask you, "How can you get me promoted?" What is your response?

a. That's a great question! I'm going to go look into all the different ways that I can get you promoted. I'll follow up with my manager and see what interviews we can get you so that you can move up. I'll put all my energy and effort into helping you get where you want to go!
b. I can try to get you some meetings with some of the higher-ups so you can gain some more exposure with them. Also, what areas are you wanting to work on to improve? We can get you on some special projects or stretch assignments that will challenge you in those areas so you can keep growing towards that promotion you want.
c. I can't get you promoted. Only you can do that, but I can certainly help guide you there. Do you know what the requirements are to get promoted? Do you know which of these requirements you meet and which ones you need to work on? Let's establish that and then I can help

you in determining your action plan to improve.

2. Donald and Jenny are both in crisis on your team. Donald has just found out that his wife has cancer. Jenny is having difficulty balancing her workloads and taking care of her terminally ill mother. Both have asked for time to meet with you today to discuss their concerns, but you don't have time to meet with both of them today. What do you do?
    a. Set a meeting with Jenny to help her find ways to prioritize so that work deadlines continue to be met. Speak with Donald and set up some time later on in the week to discuss his concerns. Provide him with any organization provided resources that might be available to him to assist with his concerns.
    b. Set a meeting with Donald and provide him with any organization provided resources that might be available to him to assist with his concerns. Speak with Jenny and set up some time later on in the week to discuss her concerns, provide her with any organization provided resources

that might be available to her to assist with her concerns.

c. Reschedule or postpone a non-urgent meeting to allow room so you can set a meeting with both Jenny and Donald that day. Provide both employees with any organization provided resources that might be available to them to assist with their concerns.

3. You have an employee on your team, Eric, that you've heard is an excellent worker, with ambition and excellent skills, but you've never seen it. Whenever you ask for something, Eric is slow to complete the tasks and tends to give you attitude. Many people on the team have informed you that Eric doesn't like you and constantly complains about you. You have a 1on1 meeting with Eric. What do you say to him?

    a. You tell Eric that you've heard he doesn't like you, and is complaining about you. Explain to him that it's not appropriate to gossip to the team, and that he needs to discontinue the behavior immediately.

    b. You tell Eric that you've heard he doesn't like you, and is complaining about you. You ask him if this is true, and what the basis is for his opinion.

c. You tell Eric that you have heard great things about his work, and that he's an excellent worker, but have sensed resistance and lack of drive when working with you. Provide Eric with examples of when you've seen this happen. Ask him if there's anything bothering him or if there's something that he wants to discuss that will assist him in returning back to that exemplary performer that others raved about.

Based on the number of A's, B's, or C's, determine your score. (If you have one of each, please read Mostly B's as this most accurately applies to you).

Novice Nurturer (mostly A's)

You have a little bit of work to do to strengthen your nurturing muscle. You tend to make decisions that aren't always taking the needs of those around you into consideration. In situations where employees question you, you tend to take full responsibility without thinking through the consequences. Read through the next chapter to see how you can continue to develop your nurturing muscle!

Moderate Nurturer (mostly B's)

You're doing a fairly good job of using your nurturing muscle, but you could use some improvement. You're able to make sound decisions and balance the needs of those around you. However, you still need to work on finding ways to manage the perceptions others have about you with a little more finesse. Read through the next chapter to see how you can continue to develop your nurturing muscle!

Strong Nurturer (mostly C's)

Congrats! You're very adept at using your nurturing muscle. You're able to balance the needs of those around you, and make decisions that support your employees and the organization you work for. You're able to manage perceptions smoothly, without negativity. Read through the next chapter to see how you can continue to develop your nurturing muscle!

Warm Up

Developing your employees

"How are you going to get me promoted?" Have you ever heard any employee say this and not known what to do? It can be daunting to feel responsible for developing your employees, but I have a secret to tell you. It's not your responsibility. Again, it's not your responsibility. How can this be?

The responsibility to develop is at the hands of your employee. Now, this isn't to say that you don't have a role in the development of your employees, but you are not in the driver seat. Think of yourself as the driver's Ed teacher. You sit in the passenger seat. You might be able to have some control over the vehicle with an emergency break, but mostly, you will be providing directions of where to go, but you won't be the one driving. Something to remember is that you are not a GPS. Although you are there to guide your employee, you are not responsible for handing them a road map of exactly how to get from point A to point B. determining the appropriate route, is up to the employee. That's your role in your employee's development.

Development roles

Let me give you some more insight as to why you role is a passenger rather than a driver. Have you ever had someone with lots of potential, but absolutely no ambition? We've all seen someone that we know could accomplish great things, if only they tried. That's the issue though; they don't want to try. No matter, how much you encourage them, or how often you try to do the work for them to set an example, if your employee isn't motivated to do the work themselves, they aren't going to do it. No amount of effort on your part is going to will it into being.

So, if the manager isn't responsible for developing the colleague, what are they responsible for?

The manager is responsible for coaching and guiding their employee towards the goals identified by the employee. How does this work?

The manager's role is to help the employee identify their career goals, and assist in them in growing their skillsets to be more competitive and prepared for their career goals, once the opportunity is available.

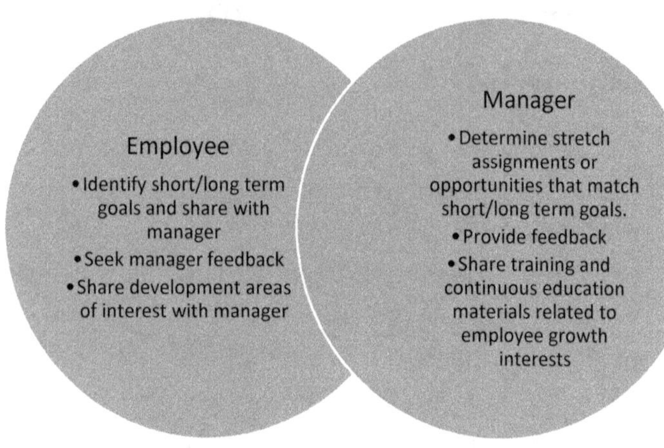

Employee and manager roles

To ensure that you're providing your employee with the proper guidance and coaching them in their development, it's important to follow the development life-cycle.

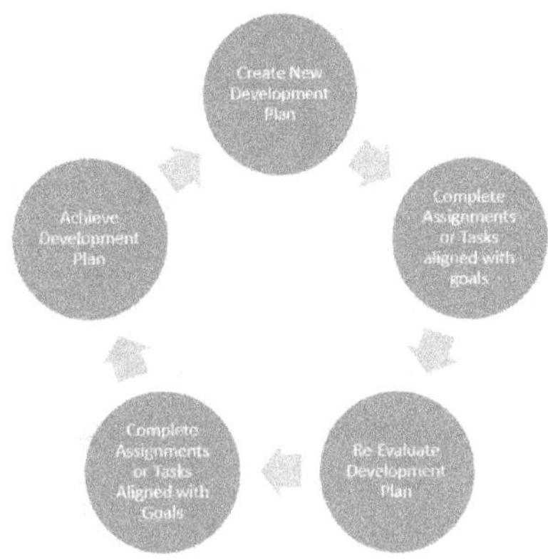

Development life-cycle

You should first work with the employee to have them create a development plan for themselves, exactly like the plan you need to make for yourself as part of your organized muscle. Many companies have forms like this with their HR or talent department. It should include the following information:

1. Short-term goals – what job and where does the employee want to be in the next 6-12 months? 1-2 years?
    a. What roles does the employee need to progress through to achieve their short-term goal?
    b. Which of these requirements does the employee currently possess and how can they further leverage those skills?
    c. Which of these requirements does the employee not currently

possess and how can they build those skills?

d. What are the minimum requirements and skillsets of the role identified in the short-term goal?

2. Long-term goals - what job and where does the employee want to be in the next 2-5 years?
    a. What roles doe the employee need to progress through to achieve their long-term goal?
    b. What are the minimum requirements and skillsets of the role identified in the long-term goal?
    c. Which of these requirements does the employee currently possess and how can they further leverage those skills?
    d. Which of these requirements does the employee not currently possess and how can they build those skills?

Once these goals have been outlined, then you can start working with the colleague to identify areas that they can leverage their strengths and develop and grow their areas of opportunity. Answering these questions will be difficult for the employee to do, which is why you want to be there to guide them.

Building these development plan goals, allows the employee to see their goals and determine logical steps to get to their ultimate goal. They will have created the roadmap for their future. Then, it's up to you to help make sure they steer themselves in the right direction. This is when you identify stretch assignments or assign responsibilities to your employee that assist them in developing the areas that they have identified that need to either be strengthened or leveraged.

Every few months, I recommend every six months, the employee should meet with you to re-evaluate their goals and track their progress towards those goals. At this time, the employee can update and revise their goals based upon the progress they have made. This cycle continues until the time comes when the employee meets their goal, whether that is obtaining a new role or receives what they were looking for. Once the employee has achieved their goal, it's time to go back to the beginning and create a new development plan because growth and development never ends!

I've found that when you correctly put the responsibility of developing onto the employee, both you and the employee feel more empowered and more energized in the development process. The employee feels in control, as they should, and the manager feels less stressed!

Understanding how to balance needs

It's a tricky business to balance all your responsibilities as a manager. There are a lot of muscles that you need to have working at the same time. You have to be able to use all your muscles and complete all your tasks. It's not an option to let one thing fall to the wayside, and even if you do, it will come back to bite you.

There are two different needs to ensure that you're balancing. The first need is your own needs. Make sure that you're taking care of yourself emotionally and physically. You are of no use to anyone if you don't make sure you're in a healthy mental state, well-fed, and rested.

One of my cardinal rules is that I take a lunch each day. Yes, there are days that I don't do that, but most days I accomplish that goal. Why is it so important I take a lunch? Do I get that hungry? No. I don't, but it's not just about eating. It's important to step away from your work for a brief amount of time to refresh yourself and re-center. If you don't do this, you end up getting burned out and being less productive overall.

In addition to taking care of your needs, you need to make sure that you're balancing the needs of your employees as well. There are a lot of times where their emotional well-being, though not part of your jurisdiction, routinely impacts you and your employees' daily work.

Some managers are of the belief that you should leave your personal issues and baggage at the door, which sounds logical… in theory. However, I've found that not only is this not possible, but it's not healthy to do. Each time an employee tries to pretend that what's going on outside of work isn't impacting them, that's exactly when their work or their attitude suffers.

First, they need to bring the issue with them, not leave it at the door. Why is that? Do I want them to bring their personal problems all to me? Do I want us to accomplish less work? No, of course not.

However, I do recognize that we're all human beings. We all have things that bother us and impact us, and pretending the problems aren't there is silly. Of course, the issue is there. And of course the issue is possibly distracting you from being able to get your work done, which typically stresses you out, and then the stress prevents you from getting work done. I call that the vicious stress cycle.

Stress cycle

Whenever I find an employee is unsuccessfully trying to keep their personal life away from their professional life and about to enter the stress cycle, I ask them to use what I call the BAM philosophy.

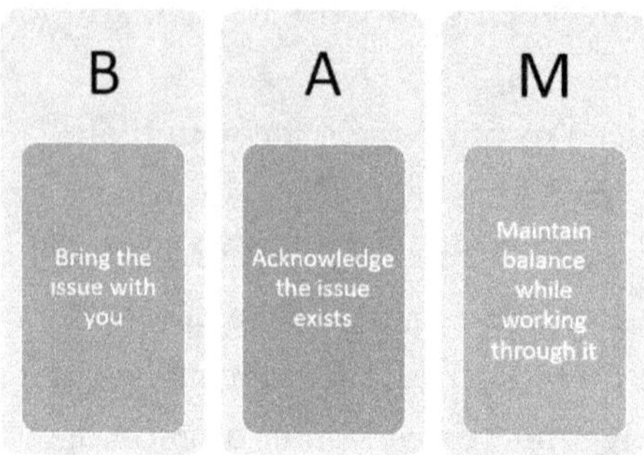

BAM philosophy

They do, in fact, need to bring the issue with them as well as acknowledge that the issue exists. Simply taking notice that the issue is there, relieves some of the fear associated with it right away. By saying, "I know it's there," the employee make a clear statement to themselves that they're not in denial and they're wanting to not let it actually impact their work.

This is much more effective than pretending that the problem is not there. Finally, the employee needs to maintain balance while working through it. This step requires sharing some aspect of what's impacting them with you, their manager. They do not need to provide details of course, but they should tell you they are experiencing issues and what their plan is to still maintain their performance while they work through their personal issue. Using this partnership method with you will give the employee the sense of being cared for and supported, which can go a very long way in helping them navigate through whatever hardship they are facing.

As a side note, be sure to use the BAM philosophy yourself as well!

Anyway, so now you're aware of your needs and of your employees' needs, but what happens if you have multiple employees with issues all at the same time and you don't have enough time available to spend assisting each employee?

Well, we know this happens. After all, it's not like employees will make sure no one else is having an issue before coming to you. Or better yet, it's not like they will wait to make sure your calendar is clear either. So, how do you balance your needs and multiple employees' needs at the same time?

Use your organized muscle! Prioritize and take it one thing at a time. As much as you may want to be a super hero, you aren't one. You are human, and can't be in multiple places at one time or help multiple people at the same time.

The best way to handle many issues at once after you prioritize them is to establish which one is more "on fire." The one that is of a more immediate need should get your assistance first. Also, if there are any items on your calendar that day that can be rescheduled, make sure to reschedule them. You'll save yourself a lot of headache.

Make sure to consider your needs, your employees' needs, and to prioritize as best you can, and you'll be in good shape for effectively managing and balancing needs.

Assessing and managing perception

One of the most elusive concepts of managing is perception. This is something that is very tough, and can never truly be mastered.

What is perception? It's what everybody *thinks* you believe or think about something, whether or not it's true. The harsh truth about perception is that perception is reality.

Whether or not you mean for someone to interpret your thoughts or actions a certain way doesn't matter. What does matter is that people do interpret what you say and do in many different ways. And, although you cannot control the way that people interpret your messages and actions, you can control how you manage those perceptions.

So what does that mean? Can't you only control your actions? How can you control the perception others have of you after the fact?

By asking and sharing your true intent.

I know that sounds horrifically simple. It may sound simple and easy, but it is not simple or easy. People often make assumptions rather than asking to confirm if they understood something. It happens consciously and unconsciously. However they are manifested though, perceptions are built on the foundation of assumption.

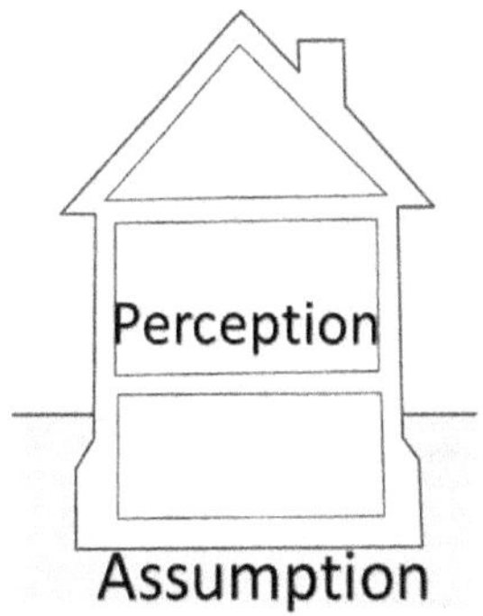

Perception and assumption

You may say or do something, but that doesn't mean that people are understanding you the way you intend them to. The only real way to know for sure is to ask if people understood you. And then after asking and receiving an answer, elaborating further on what you're hoping the employee is interpreting from your message.

But you can't just ask them, "Do you understand what I just said?" That will most definitely not work. You need to have them repeat back to you what you said, or ask a more open-ended question. Asking a yes or no question could mean you get an affirmative answer, but still not confirm whether or not the employee understood you the way you *wanted* them to understand you.

When you do ask, be sure that it's a specific and

pointed question, but be prepared to not receive the answer you're looking for. Perhaps, you might not get any answer at all, but I urge you to be vigilant and keep working at it. Perception is a tricky devil, and you have to really push through to get to the heart of the matter.

I'll give you an example of this. I was a newer manager at the time and entering a new role in an area that I had no knowledge about. I had many employees that I had inherited who reputations of being amazing, which made me had excited to work with them. One particular employee was especially revered by everyone in the organization. However, every time that I asked for something or needed something, this employee was extremely resistant to help me and sometimes downright rude to me.

I didn't understand how that could be happening. Did they have a problem with me? How could they have an issue with me after working with me for such a short time?

I'm never one to sit and wonder about something. I have always been a firm believer in asking rather than assuming. So, I asked the employee straight out.

"I've noticed that you seem resistant to work with me. When I ask for things, it feels as though you're responding in an agitated fashion. Is there something that I've said or done that has upset you?"

"No."

That was the only answer I got. For months. Finally, after continuously asking for feedback and sharing that my intent was to help and assist my employee in any way possible, the employee finally told me what was bothering them.

Several months prior they had watched me and made assumptions about how I perceived them. Based upon this, they assumed that I thought they were not an adequate employee and that I had a bad opinion of them, which is why they were not responding as professionally to me or acting as motivated. Imagine my shock when the truth was finally revealed. I was grateful to the employee for at long last sharing what had been upsetting them for all this time, but very frustrated that they couldn't just tell me that when I asked them the first time months ago.

The lesson here, is ask, ask often, and persist. You can't give up. If you think something smells, it probably does. Your instincts are spot on and most likely there is a definite reason as to why you're getting a certain response or feeling a certain way with an employee. Don't shrug it off, but rather, investigate!

Now, Workout!

It's time to test out your nurturing muscle by practicing what you've learned in real-life.

1. Think of an employee that is ambitious and looking to be promoted. Have you asked them to create a development plan

yet? Partner with them and explain their role versus your role in their development.

2. Try to remember a time where you were having difficulty balancing your personal needs with the personal and professional needs of your employees. How could you have used the BAM philosophy to address these issues?
3. Revisit a time where you were misunderstood by your employee and they formed perception of you based upon an assumption. What could you have done to circumvent the issue and prevent them from maintaining their perception for an extended period of time?

Workout Log

It's helpful to map out your ideas and plan ahead. Use these practice sheets as your guide while exercising your nurturing mental muscle.

<u>Practice: Developing your employees</u>

Think of an employee that is looking for assistance in their professional development. How can you help them grow?

Which seat of the car are you in? Which seat is your employee in?

____
____
____
____
____

What are the key roles your employee is responsible for in their career development?

____
____
____
____
____

What is your role in their development as the manager?

____
____
____
____
____

How can you guide your employee in creating a development plan?

____

____

____

____

____

How often do you want to revisit the plan with your employee?

____

____

____

____

____

<u>Practice: Understanding how to balance needs</u>

Think of an employee of yours that is facing a personal crisis that is impacting their work. How can you help them?

What is the stress cycle? How can you explain this to your employee?

____

____

____

____

____

What is the BAM Philosophy? How can you help your employee utilize it?

____

____

____

____

____

What can you do to make sure you're balancing your personal needs and the personal/professional needs of each of your employees?

____

____

____

____

____

<u>Practice: Assessing and managing perception</u>

Think of an employee that you think may have an inaccurate perception of you. What can you do to manage their perception of you?

What do you think their perception is?

____

____

____

____

____

What was your intent?

____

____

____

____

____

How can you elaborate on your true intent with your employee?

____

____

____

____

____

What follow up can you have with your employee to make sure they truly understand your intent and rid themselves of their past assumption?

____

____

____

____

____

Cool Down

Now, you're equipped to be more nurturing than ever!

By understanding the development roles of you and your employee as well as which activities are your responsibility versus your employee's responsibility, you'll be able to actively assist your employee in developing towards their personal and professional goals. You can help your employee to determine their skillsets in order to draft a self-development plan that outlines their short and long-term goals. By following the development life-cycle, your employee will be able to see their goals clearly and work to achieve them with your guidance.

You're now able to balance the needs of your personal life, as well as the personal/professional needs of your employees, while also ensuring you prioritize everything when there's more work than time to handle everything.

Ultimately, you're able to see when an inaccurate perception may have been formed about you, and have the tools to ask for clarification, elaborate on your true intent, and re-define the understanding your employee should have about you.

Through the use of your nurturing muscle, you'll be able to forge strong bonds with your employees while helping them and yourself maintain a healthy work/life balance.

7 GENUINE MUSCLE

Definition

Genuine: Being what something or someone appears or claims to be; real, not false (McIntosh, 2013).

Workout Objectives

To be an effective manager, you need to build your mental muscle and become genuine in your communication and actions.

After this workout you'll be stronger at:

- Being transparent and credible
- Demonstrating active listening
- Providing balanced feedback

Stretching

Let's see how genuine you are right now with this short quiz.

1. You have just found out from executive leadership that you'll be downsizing the organization. You've been instructed not to say anything to your employees at this time, until all those being laid off have been privately informed first. However,

as usual, one of the people who was let go contacts someone who is not getting let go and the information spreads across the entire floor. One of your employees approaches you and asks you if you know about what's going on. How do you respond?

a. You tell the employee that you have no idea what they are talking about and to not listen to gossip. You ask them to return back to work.
b. You tell the employee that you do know and that there's a small collection of people being laid off due to downsizing, but to please keep the information confidential until it's formally announced.
c. You tell the employee that you have been provided with information regarding what they are asking about, but are not allowed to disclose any information or details at this time, however, you will share information as soon as you are cleared to do so. Ask the employee to please remain calm and not to share any information they receive. A formal

announcement with official and accurate information will be shared when possible.

2. You have an assignment that you're working on with a tight deadline. You are behind on the assignment because of other projects that have taken priority until now. You have very limited time to complete this project, when you receive a phone call from one of your employees asking if they can get your advice on something very important to them, which is quite urgent. What do you do?
    a. Tell them to go ahead and tell you what's going on. As they share the information with you, you continue to work on the project so that you don't get behind.
    b. You tell them that you have limited time, but to go ahead and share with you what's on their mind. As they share the information with you, you continue to work on the project so that you don't get behind.
    c. You tell the employee that you have ten minutes at this time to talk with them, but then you'll need to continue working on a

time sensitive project. Schedule follow up time to talk with the employee if ten minutes isn't sufficient. If the employee wants to talk for ten minutes, do not work on the project and focus on the employee and what they are saying.

3. Ted is an employee that meets expectations. He does what is asked, and typically doesn't struggle with completing his tasks. Recently, Ted has been trying to improve his performance to exceed expectations. He has been handling more projects and sharing his input more regularly in meetings. However, Ted is also being negative during meetings and not phrasing things productively. You are about to have a 1on1 meeting with Ted. What do you tell him?
    a. Tell Ted that he's not phrasing things productively in the team meeting, and if his goal is truly to move up in the company, he needs to work on finding more diplomatic ways to share his thoughts. Ask if he understands, and conclude the meeting.
    b. Tell Ted that he's a valued member of the team, but that he's

phrasing things negatively and needs to work on that. However, you can see that he's really trying to improve this performance, and it's being noticed, and is looking good! Ask if he understands, and conclude the meeting.

c. Tell Ted that you've been seeing him trying to make efforts to really enhance his performance. Based upon that, you wanted to go over some strengths and some opportunities with him so he can keep working towards the promotion he's interested in. Tell Ted that he's doing a great job of taking on additional work and continuing to balance his other tasks. Continue this as this is going great! One opportunity to focus on is to making sure he's phrasing things productively in the meetings. Provide a few examples and share some more diplomatic ways he could have shared his views. Ask if he understands, and conclude the meeting.

Based on the number of A's, B's, or C's, determine your score. (If you have one of each, please read Mostly B's as this most accurately applies to you).

Novice Genuineness (mostly A's)

You have a little bit of work to do to strengthen your genuine muscle. Currently, you are afraid to be transparent, and aren't focusing on listening to your employees. You also tend to focus on the constructive feedback and forget to share the positive feedback with your employees. Take a look over the next chapter to see ways that you can further enhance your genuine mental muscle!

Moderate Genuineness (mostly B's)

You're doing a fairly good job of using your genuine muscle, but you could use some improvement. You're able to provide more balanced feedback and are trying to be an active listener, but be careful not to hide your constructive information within positive feedback. You'll also want to be sure that by being transparent, you're also not breaking confidentiality. Take a look over the next chapter to see ways that you can further enhance your genuine mental muscle!

Strong Genuineness (mostly C's)

Congrats! You're very adept at using your genuine muscle. You're able to listen actively, speak with credibility and transparency, while also sharing balanced feedback with your employees. Take a look over the next chapter to see ways that you can further enhance your genuine mental muscle!

Warm Up

Being transparent and credible

Transparency is something that many managers either fear or avoid. What if the employee knows too much? How will that impact the bottom line of productivity?

Well, I hate to tell you this, but if you're worried that your employee knows something, I can almost guarantee they already do.

Hiding truths from your employees or full-on lying to your employees can have some very serious ramifications. By cultivating a culture of mistrust, your employees may not come to you when issues arise because they don't feel you have their best interests or your customer's best interest at heart.

Another serious ramification of being non-transparent is that employees will not try as hard if they feel that their manager is dishonest. Much like the buy-in process for the strategic muscle, being transparent and credible encourages your employees to give their best efforts. When the employee understands the bigger picture and the greater cause, they are much more likely to give their all to that cause. So, by being dishonest or non-transparent, you run the risk of losing overall productivity from your employees.

And if that information isn't compelling enough or you, it's also important for me to mention that being transparent and honest is just the right thing to do.

What's too honest? What if you're specifically instructed to withhold information or to wait to share information until further direction is received?

These are all good questions. Although, you may need to delay when you share a message with an employee because you're specifically instructed to do so, that doesn't mean you need to lie to the employee as a result.

I'll give you an example. Let's say that you've been told by your manager that the branding of the company is changing, and as a result, some of the people from the marketing team are being laid off. However, until those marketing team employees are informed, you should not be sharing that message with any of your employees.

So, what do you do if one of your employees finds out and ask you point blank if it's true? Do you tell the truth and break confidentiality? Or do you lie and possibly endanger your credibility with your employee?

The answer is that you do neither. You don't want to break confidentiality, but you also do not want to deny knowing what is going to happen. The alternative? Tell, what I call the allowed truth.

- Share what you are allowed to share
- Confirm that you have more information
- Explain you are not yet allowed to share
- Ask the employee to stand by until additional direction is shared

Allowed truth alternative

Share that you've been made aware of information that affects marketing. Indicate that you are not permitted to disclose that information at this time, but will share it as soon as you are given permission do so.

This way you're being honest, but you aren't breaking confidentiality. This also is a great opportunity to ask them to respect confidentiality as well and not continue to spread the information until accurate information is shared and disseminated with everyone.

People often think that if something is "need to know" that means that you should tell those who are not allowed to know the opposite of the truth. That's both damaging to your reputation and also completely unnecessary.

I've found that by sharing the allowed truth, you're solidifying the trust between you and your employee as well as the trust between you and your manager.

In addition to sharing the allowed truth, there is one more behavior that you must exhibit in order to demonstrate transparency and be credible, which goes beyond being honest.

You must keep your promises, or don't make promises you won't be able to keep. Follow through on your actions. Don't tell an employee that you are going to do something unless you are absolutely sure that you're going to be able to do it. Much like a doctor doesn't promise that he'll be able to cure an employee's illness, neither should you promise to do something for your employee that you can't be certain of.

For example, if you promise your employee that you will meet with them to discuss their development plan, and then never follow through with that, you have lost credibility with your employee.

Now, of course, we all have great intent, and sometimes, we just can't foresee that we won't be able to follow through on something we promised. It happens, but you have to take ownership of that and acknowledge the fact you won't be able to make good on your promise.

So, keeping the example going, you promise that you'll go over the development plan with your employee, but find out that a new meeting was scheduled that you have to attend. Instead of just cancelling the meeting and saying nothing to the employee, try to reschedule the meeting. Take the time to circle back with the employee and explain that a new request has been made of you that you're required to attend so you'll need to reschedule the meeting. This will show the employee that you do follow through, but when you can't, that you will be honest and up-front about it.

Although you can reschedule, make sure that you don't make a habit of this. If you always reschedule and never attend something, that's about as bad as it would have been to cancel the meeting in the first place. Do your best to reschedule something no more than two times. Doing more so that that can impact your credibility and the trust your employee has in you.

By using the allowed truth approach and making sure to follow through on your promises, you'll ensure that you are both transparent and credible, which will reap benefits of mutual trust and potentially increased performance from your employees.

Demonstrating active listening

Everyone wants to feel heard. It's an intrinsic need that we all have. If we feel like we're not being heard we typically get angry and act out or get sad and withdraw. Both alternatives aren't something you want to see in your employees.

Eye contact is typically the main thing people use to demonstrate they are listening, but that just doesn't cut it anymore. Just because you're looking at someone, doesn't mean that you're actively listening to them.

Also, in today's age of technology, you don't always get to communicate in-person. Often, when you don't see the person, you're even less likely to remain engaged in the conversation and actively listen.

What can you do to make sure that you're really listening to your employee? SIT!

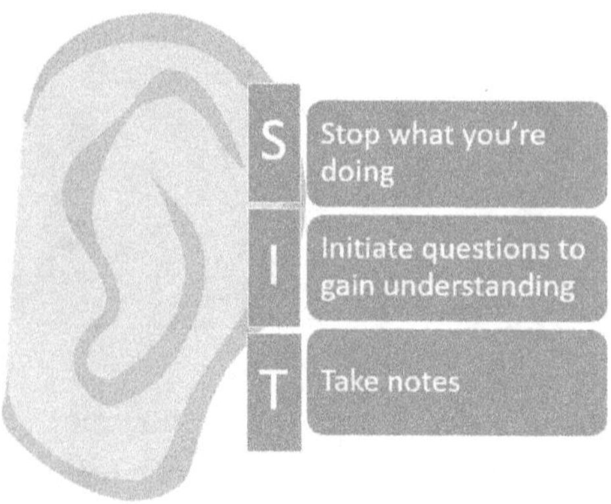

SIT approach to active listening

Using the SIT method will allow you to really hone in on what your employee is trying to tell you. Stop what you're doing. This doesn't mean, stop some of what you're doing, it means to stop all of what you're doing. Give your entire focus to your employee. This is difficult to do. We as managers have so much to do and not a lot of time to do it. We're all guilty of not actively listening, but do you want to can to eliminate all the other items and give your full attention to the person you speaking with. After all, that's what you want when you're speaking with someone, right?

After you've stopped everything you were doing, it's also important to initiate questions. Ask probing questions to better understand what the employee is telling you. You also want to ask questions to make sure you're understanding them correctly.

A word to the wise though. Asking questions, doesn't mean pepper the person with questions and continually interrupt them with questions just to show you're listening. That can cause the employee to feel like you're not listening because it seems like all you want to do is ask questions to make it appear as if you're listening. It came seem like all you're doing is waiting for your turn to speak.

Also, be wary of trying to empathize too much with your employee. What I mean is, don't try to share a story about yourself to demonstrate you understand until you're sure the employee has finished sharing what they wanted to share. If you interrupt and try to empathize to early, you run the risk of sounding like an egomaniac who only likes to talk about their stories.

After you've asked questions, you also might want to take notes, which means writing down questions here as well. If you have a question, but don't want to interrupt, taking a note down of what you want to ask is a good alternative to make sure you're not interrupting, but ensuring you remember the question you want to ask when it is appropriate.

If you use the SIT method, you'll be able to effectively listen actively and demonstrate to your employee that they are a priority to you, which will not only build rapport with your employee, but also gain their respect.

Providing balanced feedback

Giving feedback to your employees is a very instrumental part of your job. With your strategic muscle you've learned how to hold your employee accountable. Through your transformative muscle, you've acquired the ability to adapt your message so that it meets the needs or your employee and change hats to fit the situation. With the help of your resolute muscle you know how to handle difficult conversations and give in-the-moment feedback. You have almost everything you need, but how do you make sure that you've giving balanced feedback to your employee?

It's not possible to give 50/50 feedback of positive versus constructive feedback, mostly because people are not consistently doing an equal amount of good to not so good behaviors or performance.

There are lot of opinions out there about what ratio of positive to constructive feedback you should give to your employees, but I don't think that makes any sense. Do you know why? I don't keep a mathematic tracker of my feedback to make sure I'm staying within the defined ratio.

So, what should you do instead? Focus on ensuring that you give both strengths and opportunities while meeting with your employee. It doesn't mean you should make something up if you have a lot of constructive things to share. It does mean that you need to think about what items that employee does contribute and call attention to that, as well as ask them to find additional ways to use that strength to assist them with their opportunity.

Now, when I say you want to give both positive and constructive feedback, I do *not* mean that you should do the "feedback sandwich," which is a very well known, and very widely discouraged approach to providing feedback.

What's the feedback sandwich? It's when you take a constructive feedback item and hide it between two positive feedback items.

Here's an example.

"Jenny, you did a great job on that status report last week! Next time though, could you make sure to submit it on time? We missed our deadline by a day. But overall, really good job. It looked great!"

The reason this is bad is because the message is lost. The employee will most likely only hear the positive comments, and might fully overlook the constructive comments.

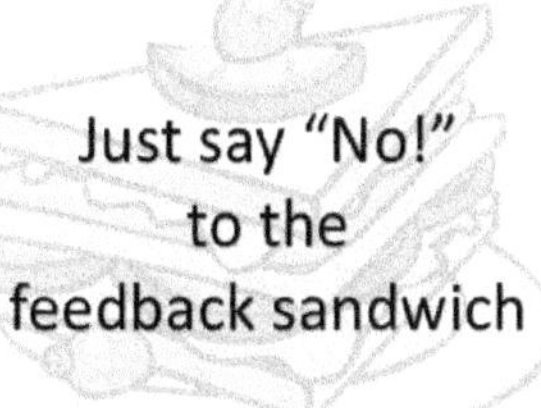

Feedback sandwich

Instead of making a feedback sandwich, try to provide comments, but keep them separate. Remember, that constructive feedback doesn't have to be overly pleasant, but it also shouldn't be sugar-coated.

I also recommend that you seek the employee's self-evaluation prior to giving them your comments. It's good to see how well the employee is able to self-assess, and provides you with a potential opportunity to reiterate their viewpoints or re-direct them to a more accurate understanding.

However, it's also very possible the employee has no idea how to self-assess. This is why you always want to ask the employee to try to self-assess so you can help them hone this very essential skill in personal development.

Here's an example.

"Jenny, I wanted to talk to you about the results of the project from last week. There were some strengths and opportunities that came out of it. What did you think went well?"

"Well, I think that I came into it with a lot of excitement. I felt really good about it."

"Great! So, Jenny, was there anything you think you could have improved while working on this?"

"Not really. I did my best."

"I definitely agree with you about your excitement. A great strength of yours was your attitude on this. I really enjoyed your enthusiasm and your vigor while working on it. Keep that going for future projects. As an opportunity though, you'll want to make sure that you complete the project on time. You missed the deadline, and we can't have our information being shared last minute in the future. Do you have any idea of what you could do next time to avoid missing the deadline?"

By following this method, you're seeking the employee's feedback about how they can improve their area of opportunity. By separating out and identifying a strength and an opportunity, you're calling attention to everything in a balanced way, to prevent the employee from only hearing what they want to hear, at least as much as you can. There is always the possibility they employee isn't actively listening and might not get your message, but that's not completely in your control.

What if the employee didn't do anything good or didn't do anything bad? How do you remain balanced in those situations?

If the employee didn't do anything good on the item you're discussing with them, I would challenge you to dig deeper. Everyone has redeeming qualities and does something well. Look a little further, and if needed, seek the input of a peer or your manager to assist with finding a strength.

In the event the employee didn't do anything bad to provide constructive feedback on, that's great! This doesn't mean that you don't ask for areas of opportunity though. There are always ways for us to improve and grow, no matter what. So, instead of providing an area that didn't go well, try to share an area that you would like to see them continue to hone or grow so they can keep moving in their career development plan.

As you can see, providing balanced feedback, doesn't have to be complicated or hard. And although you want to give feedback to your employees, encourage your employee to not only wait for you to provide them with feedback, but also to actively seek it from you and from their peers. Feedback is very powerful, and everyone should take the initiative to seek information rather than waiting for someone to give it to them.

Now, Workout!

It's time to test out your genuine muscle by practicing what you've learned in real-life.

1. Think of a time that you were asked a question by an employee and weren't sure how to respond to their question. What could you have said to use the allowed truth approach? What could you have done to be transparent and credible?
2. Remember a time that you had a conversation with an employee where you weren't completely focused on the employee. How could you use the SIT

method to improve your active listening skills in that situation?

3. Look back on a feedback session that you had with an employee. Was it balanced? How could you have provided balanced feedback as well as sought their feedback during the process as well?

Workout Log

It's helpful to map out your ideas and plan ahead. Use these practice sheets as your guide while exercising your genuine mental muscle.

Practice: Being transparent and credible

Think of a time that you were asked a question by an employee and weren't sure what to say. How should you respond?

What is the allowed truth you could share?

____

____

____

____

____

Did you make a promise that you couldn't keep? How can you avoid doing that?

____

____

____

____

____

How could you follow through with your employee, but also maintain appropriate confidentiality?

____

____

____

____

____

<u>Practice: Demonstrating active listening</u>

Think of a time that you didn't give your full attention to something your employee was telling you. What could you have done differently?

How could the SIT method have improved your active listening skills?

____

____

____

____

____

What questions could you have asked to gain more understanding?

____

____

____

____

____

<u>Practice: Providing balanced feedback</u>

What's a feedback session that you need to have with an employee? How do you want to share this with them?

What is a strength you want them to be aware of?

____

____

____

____

____

What is an opportunity you want them to be aware of?

____

____

____

____

____

How can you elicit their feedback during this conversation?

____
____
____
____

Cool Down

Now, you're equipped to be more genuine than ever!

You can use the allowed truth message to share information with your employees to gain trust with your employee but also maintain confidentiality and respect with your manager.

It's important to follow through on promises you make and provide explanations for why you're not able to keep a promise, if you are unable to follow though.

You will be more genuine by using the SIT method and actively listening to your employee. Take it to heart, and stop what you're doing, initiate questions to gain understanding, and possibly take notes.

You're also able to provide balanced feedback where you avoid the feedback sandwich and embrace the balance of providing a strength, and opportunity, and seeking the employee's self-assessment.

All of these behaviors and activities will build trust with your employee and demonstrate that you are genuine and want to support your employees to the best of your ability.

8 BE STRONG

Definition

Strong: effective; of a good quality or level and likely to be successful (McIntosh, 2013).

Workout Objectives

To be an effective manager it's important to have a balance in all the mental muscles that make you STRONG.

After this workout you'll be stronger at:

- Putting all the muscles to work
- Continually challenging your muscles
- Sharing the knowledge forward

Stretching

Let's see how STRONG you've become in this short quiz.

1. You're in a meeting with Eddie, who tends to not take feedback well. Eddie has been negative about a change to protocol that took place. You're having a conversation with Eddie about how he's been negative recently. He immediately changes the subject and tells you about how you're a terrible manager and he has no respect for you. What do you do?

a. Tell Eddie that you do not appreciate his tone and ask him to be more respectful. Stay on task, and tell him you're here today to discuss his negativity and need to have an action plan of how he will change his behavior.
b. Let Eddie know that you do hear him. Ask him if he said he feels that you're not managing him properly. After getting his opinions shared, explain that you'll set up some separate time to discuss some ways that the two of you can better communicate together. Once you establish that with him, ask him why he has been acting so negatively about the changes on the team recently.
c. Explain why the changes took place to Eddie, and ask him if he is would be able to help with choosing a specific way to handle the changes. After having that discussion, let Eddie know that you do hear him. Ask him if he said he feels that you're not managing him properly. After getting his opinions shared, explain that you'll set up some separate time to discuss some ways that the two of you can better communicate together. Once you establish that with him, ask him why he has been acting so negatively

about the changes on the team recently. After the meeting with Eddie, take some time to think about the feedback he provided you and come up with a way to address his concerns. Share this with him in your follow up conversation with him.

2. You need to have a conversation with your team about changing a major process. How do you prepare?
    a. Take time to plan out your message to the team. Create a presentation and share it with a team explaining the change, what is going to happen, and why it is going to happen, and what you expect of everyone as you progress through the changes.
    b. Take time to plan out your message to the team. Create a presentation and share it with a team explaining the change, what is going to happen, and why it is going to happen, and what you expect of everyone as you progress through the changes. Determine some options that the team can choose between in the process, and get the team's opinion on which option they want to use.
    c. Take time to plan out your message to the team. Create a presentation and share it with a team explaining the change, what is going to happen, and

why it is going to happen, and what you expect of everyone as you progress through the changes. Be prepared to change mentality based upon the reactions and responses from your team.

3. Your employee, Amber, has been disruptive on the team. You want to speak with her in a timely fashion, but know this will be a difficult conversation that you're worried about because you want to be sure you're treating Amber the way you would with anyone else on the team.
    a. Repeat the manager mantra to yourself. Think of how you would want to be talked to, if this were you, and then think about how you would handle the situation with a different employee. Set up time to speak with Amber right away, and have the conversation with her.
    b. Think through the situation objectively, looking for patterns, seeking feedback from your manager, and then craft the message you want to share with Amber. Repeat the manager mantra to yourself. Think of how you would want to be talked to, if this were you, and then think about how you would handle the situation with a different employee. Set up time

to speak with Amber right away, and have the conversation with her.

c. Think through the situation objectively, looking for patterns, seeking feedback from your manager, and then craft the message you want to share with Amber. Repeat the manager mantra to yourself. Think of how you would want to be talked to, if this were you, and then think about how you would handle the situation with a different employee. Remove any obstacles that are preventing you from having the conversation with her timely, then set up time to speak with Amber right away, and have the conversation with her.

4. You've been in meetings all day and just looked at your email, which is overflowing with items that you need to handle. You immediately feel overwhelmed. What do you do?
   a. Go through your email and respond to items chronologically unless it will take you longer than five minutes to handle. Move on through the rest of your emails, returning to those items once you've been able to handle them.
   b. Go through your email and respond to items chronologically unless it will take you longer than five minutes to handle. Move on through the rest of

your emails, returning to those items once you've been able to handle them. If you don't have time to address the issues today, set a reminder in your calendar to handle them the next day.

c. Look at your calendar for the rest of the day today and tomorrow to determine when you'll have time to review all these items. Block off time in your calendar to review your email. Once that time arrives, go through your email and respond to items chronologically unless it will take you longer than five minutes to handle. Move on through the rest of your emails, returning to those items once you've been able to handle them. File emails into folders or flag them using your color coding system. If you don't have time to address the issues today, set a reminder in your calendar to handle them the next day.

5. You have two employees that have requested an emergency meeting with you. Pam wants to discuss her career path with you and how she can move up in the company. Alex wants to meet with you to discuss something personal. Your calendar is already booked up. What do you do?

   a. Look at your calendar, and reschedule items that can be moved to a later date. Block out time to speak with both Pam and Alex. When meeting with Pam, see what she wants to discuss and determine what to do after talking to her. When speaking with Alex, listen, but then tell him that he needs to seek professional assistance with a therapist.

b. Look at your calendar, and reschedule items that can be moved to a later date. Block out time to speak with both Pam and Alex. When meeting with Pam, help her begin creating a development plan so she can determine what her short and long-term goals are. With that information, then you'll be able to identify which skillsets she needs to grow in order to further her career. When speaking with Alex, listen, but then tell him that he needs to seek professional assistance with a therapist.

c. Look at your calendar, and reschedule items that can be moved to a later date. Block out time to speak with both Pam and Alex. When meeting with Pam, help her begin creating a development plan so she can determine what her short and long-term goals are. With that information, then you'll be able to identify which skillsets she needs to grow in order to further her career. When speaking with Alex, listen to his concerns. Remind him to recognize that this will impact his work and think of realistic solutions to help him maintain his work while working through his personal issues. Then recommend that he seek professional assistance with a therapist.

6. You have been approached by a frustrated employee, Brad, who has heard that other employees are getting promoted over him. You know this, but a formal announcement hasn't been made and you are not allowed to share any of this information with him. What do you do?
    a. Stop what you're doing and listen to what Brad is saying. Ask him additional questions to understand his concerns. Take some notes of the comments he's providing you. Then tell him that you're not allowed to speak with him about his concerns, and to please not share the information with others.
    b. Stop what you're doing and listen to what Brad is saying. Ask him additional questions to understand his concerns. Take some notes of the comments he's providing you. Then tell him that you'll follow up with him once you get information. Mark your

calendar to remind yourself to speak with him.

c. Stop what you're doing and listen to what Brad is saying. Ask him additional questions to understand his concerns. Take some notes of the comments he's providing you. Explain to him that you understand he is frustrated, however, you're not authorized to speak with him about it. Instead, let's discuss what it will take to get him recognized for his talents. Ask him to update his development plan and setup some additional time in a few weeks to go over it together.

Based on the number of A's, B's, or C's, determine your score. (If you a tie, please read Mostly B's as this most accurately applies to you).

Novice at STRONG (mostly A's)

You have a little bit of work to do to strengthen your mental muscles. You're thinking along the lines of the STRONG methods, but are still falling back on old habits. Read on to find ways to enhance your skillsets.

Moderate at STRONG (mostly B's)

You're doing a fairly good job of using your mental muscles, but you could use some improvement. Although you are doing a good job of identifying which muscle to use and finding the approach or method that will help, sometimes you're still shying away from having the tough conversations. Read on to find ways to enhance your skillsets.

STRONG! (Mostly C's)

Congrats! You're very adept at using your mental muscles. You know what muscle to use and you're finding the appropriate method or approach to use. You're bold, and unafraid to dive in and handle the situation. Read on to find ways to enhance your skillsets.

Warm Up

Putting all the muscles to work

You've learned about all the mental muscles. There are a lot of useful skills within the STRONG model that will allow you to be a more effective manager, but there are a lot of different methods and models within STRONG. How will you know what to do and when to do it? Will you be able to tell which muscle you should use and when you should use it?

I have confidence in you. My answer is yes! You can also use the 3 S's to remind you of how to address your problem.

3 S's approach

Initially, no matter what, you'll need to identify the situation that you're in. Determine exactly what it is that you're working with. I find that writing everything down can be helpful, so write down the who, what, where, when, how, and why. Once you've taken stock of the situation, you can move onto the next S.

What skillsets do you need for this? Figure out what areas this is impacted by. By narrowing down to the particular skillsets, you'll then be able to move onto the next step.

To get a solution, you made a list of the situation,

determined the skillset you need, which means you'll be able to identify the muscle that is needed to assist with the situation. By figuring out what muscle you need, now you can go to the at particular muscle and remind yourself of what methods would assist you. Then, use the tools provided within that muscle, and start using them.

Not feeling super confident yet? That's okay. You'll have some practice in your workout and workout log.

But, because I care, we'll do an example together.

First, we'll figure out the situation. I've included a sample Situation outline below.

Who: Your employee, Ben. He typically meets expectations and has been relatively open to feedback in the past. He is widely respected and listened to by his peers.
What: Ben has been acting out and making negative comments about the latest project the team has been assigned to work.
Where: Ben has been displaying this behavior during team meetings and among his teammates in their cubicles and offices.
When: Ben started acting out over the past two weeks. It has been increasing in severity.
How: Ben is communicating this verbally and also, you've had a few emails forwarded to that demonstrate he has been writing negative information as well.

Why: It seems that Ben is not happy with his role or that he is happy with the new project the team has been assigned, but you are not sure.

You've determined the situation. Now, it's time to make a list of the skillsets that would be needed to address this situation.

Skillsets

- Holding others accountable
- Managing through change
- Demonstrating flexibility
- Wearing different hats
- Handling difficult conversations
- Assessing and managing perception

Great! Now we know what the situation is as well as the skillsets needed to handle it. What now? Well, we have identified the skillsets, but now we have to figure out which muscles and exercises would apply to those skillsets. We're not quite ready with a solution just yet. So, taking the skillsets, we'll narrow it down further to identify which models and approaches would fit this particular case.

Skillsets

- Holding others accountable – S
- Managing through change – T
- Demonstrating flexibility – T

- Wearing different hats – T
- Handling difficult conversations - R
- Assessing and managing perception – N

We've identified that we're going to need to use our strategic, transformative, resolute, and nurturing muscles to take control of this issue. Let's go even further and determine what models and approaches from those muscles would apply here and what about them we'll want to use for handling the situation with Ben.

Skillsets

- Holding others accountable
    - ARCS – need to prepare for Ben taking us off topic when bringing up his recent behavioral changes.
- Managing through change
    - Use the three steps for managing through change – need to explain the whys and the options to Ben as he doesn't seem bought into the new process. Currently, Ben is an Adversarial Anchor, so we'll want to get him more involved in the project to gain his buy-in as well.
- Demonstrating flexibility
    - Determine the content, method, and audience for the message – Ben responds well to face-to-face feedback

when possible, so should have in-person conversation and be direct. Ben doesn't like when you tip-toe around the issue.

- Wearing different hats
    - Will most likely need the manager, therapist, and facilitator hats to get Ben back on the right track.
- Handling difficult conversations
    - Need to use three steps to difficult conversations – Ben might get defensive during this conversation, so we'll want to repeat the manager mantra to gain confidence, as well as look at what we would respond best to as well as how we would approach this if we were talking to someone other than Ben.
- Assessing and managing perception
    - We're not sure why Ben is suddenly behaving this way, we should ask. We don't want to assume that we know what his issue is.

At this point, can take the information from above to form a solution. We've come up with some solid ways to address the situation with Ben. We've established that we are going to have an in-person conversation where we will ask him what's going on with him as we've seen a significant change in his demeanor. After hearing from him, we'll also want to explain the changes that are happening. Tell him why they are happening and see what options we can offer him so he can participate in the change, and buy-in to the new updates. We also know to prepare ourselves for the conversation with Ben by repeating the manager mantra, identifying some options to provide Ben, as well as preparing to use the ARCS method in the conversation, if necessary.

Great job! See? That wasn't so bad. You successfully went through a case study of how to take all these mental muscles and use them together to be an effective manager.

Continually challenging your muscles

It's great that you now know how to use your mental muscles. The great news is that you don't have to memorize these strategies either. You can revisit them whenever you need to as you continue to grow in confidence and skill.

I have a few recommendations for you use these skills. The first recommendation is to be bold. Don't hold back because you're afraid of what might happen. You never know what will happen unless you put yourself out there.

And, if you really are afraid to do something, I recommend that you use the worst case scenario method.

Worst case scenario method

What I mean by this, is picture the absolutely most horrible thing that you're afraid could happen. Really think about it. What's the worst thing that could come out of what you fear? Is that something you can live with? Most of the time, you'll find that once you've identified what really is making you afraid, you won't be as afraid anymore.

The next suggestion is to try new things. Just because you haven't done something before, doesn't mean it shouldn't be something you try now. Within reason of course!

And finally, don't be afraid to fail. I know that it can be very upsetting to think of failing, but ultimately, failure is what leads to innovation. People don't discover excellence after only trying something once. So, keep going. Don't give up!

<u>Sharing the knowledge forward</u>

I hope that you find these tools useful, and that you always challenge yourself to use your muscles and improve. I also hope that you don't stop there. Please take what you're learned and share it with others.

Why would I ask you to do it rather than pedaling my own book on the masses? Well, that would be great too, but teachers tend to learn the material even better once they start lecturing and sharing what they've learned. So, if you really want to get better at using your mental muscles, teach it to someone. You'll be surprised at how much more information you will absorb.

Teaching others has its benefits in helping you, but it also has the added benefit of creating the next generation of managers. We need to have skilled people ready to take over and lead the group. Take someone under your wing and show them how they too can be an effective manager.

Even if someone on your team, doesn't want to be a manager, that doesn't mean that these muscles go unused. You should be just as motivated to teach those who don't want to be managers. The tools and methods we talked about relate to everyone. You can use them in managing, but you can also apply them to your daily life even if you aren't in a managerial role.

Now, Workout!

It's time to test out your mental muscles by practicing what you've learned in real-life.

1. Think about an issue that you've been struggling with handling. How can you

use the mental muscles to approach the situation? Use the 3 S's to help you determine what to do.

2. Think about some ways that you can challenge yourself to use the mental muscles daily. What are some ways that you can make sure you don't just read this and not use what you've learned?
3. Who is someone on your team that you can share this knowledge with? What ideas and methods could benefit them in their career growth?

Workout Log

It's helpful to map out your ideas and plan ahead. Use these practice sheets as your guide while exercising your mental muscles.

<u>Practice: Putting all the muscles to work</u>

Think of work situation that you've been afraid to address. How can you use the mental muscles and be STRONG to handle it? What's the situation?

Who?

____

____

____

____

____

What?

____

____

____

____

____

Where?

____

____

____

____

____

When?

____

____

____

____

____

How?

Why?

What skillsets will you need to handle this situation?

Which muscles are these for?

What methods or approaches make sense for this?

____

____

____

____

____

What is your solution?

____

____

____

____

____

<u>Practice: Continually challenging your muscles</u>

What are some ways you can use your mental muscles today?

____

____

____

____

____

How do you want to challenge yourself to use your mental muscles in the next 6 months?

____

____

____

____

____

What's a stretch goal for yourself in using your mental muscles?

____

____

____

____

____

Practice: Sharing the knowledge forward

Who is someone on your team that could benefit from this knowledge?

____

____

____

____

____

What lessons do you want to teach them?

____

____

____

____

____

How could you share this information with them?

____

____

____

____

____

What lessons would you like to learn better by sharing this with your employee?

____

____

____

____

____

Cool Down

Now, you're equipped to be STRONG! You did it! You've learned how to determine the situation, identify the skillsets needed, and create a solution that will handle the situation appropriately.

It's important to understand the muscles for yourself, but to continually challenge yourself to go outside your comfort zone, and test your mental muscles in different atmospheres.

Don't keep this knowledge to yourself. Share it with people on your team. Give them guidance and help them use it to better themselves and how they interact with others whether or not management is a career goal for them.

9 WHAT NOW?

Just like any work out, you're never truly done challenging yourself, but now you have an understanding of what it takes to manage with purpose. Don't just read this once and never look at it again. Treat it as your daily management handbook. Use it with every decision you make, especially the ones that you find are difficult to make.

Be Strategic. Work to gain buy-in from your employees by explaining the whys and sharing options with them. Hold them accountable to their actions, and remember that it's up to the employee to redirect their behaviors positively or negatively. And remember to manage your emotions, understand that there's a specific time and place that you have to have your own responses, and that the time is never in front of your employees.

Be Transformative. Show that you can adapt to change and be flexible. Operate as the leader that navigates the team through change and changes hats and mindsets to fit the situation.

Be Resolute. Stay firm in your decisions, and feel confident in what you do by being consistent, having those difficult conversations when they're warranted, and providing in-the-moment feedback.

Be Organized. Make a plan and set up methods so you can manage your time wisely. Set short and long-term goals for yourself. Plan ahead and be proactive so that you're the one at the front of things, rather than lagging behind.

Be Nurturing. Develop your employees to be the best they can be, and help them determine their dreams and goals. Find ways to balance everyone's needs and be sure that you're addressing reality rather than just operating under assumptions based off of perception.

Be Genuine. Set a positive example of transparency and credibility with everyone around you. Listen actively when people are speaking with you, and when you provide feedback, ensure that you're being honest and balanced.

S	Strategic
T	Transformative
R	Resolute
O	Organized
N	Nurturing
G	Genuine

STRONG Model

Challenge yourself to revisit these ideas a week, a month, or even a year from now. Why would I say that? It's not like I can rewrite the whole book for you to learn something new, right? Wrong! The ideas within this book might not change, but you will. You will continue to grow, change, and adapt your management style to fit the needs of those around you and your own needs. Come back to this and revisit it. You'll find that some of your muscles have grown strong and may have even become second nature. Just like working out other muscles, maybe you enjoy one workout more than another, but that doesn't mean you don't want to work them all out.

You'll also find that some of the muscles have atrophied over time because you're not using them. Perhaps it's the "abs" workout of your mental muscles. I call it an abs workout, because it's hard to do, no fun, and you feel like you never see results. I promise you though, keep at it. Keep testing it, and even if you don't feel like you're seeing results, know that they are there.

I remember a time when I was at my wits end with my team. I felt as though I was putting so much effort into them, into giving them what they wanted, and putting everything that I had into trying to make sure they were empowered to do their work in their own ways. Yet, I was more tired, frustrated, and disengaged than ever. I had never felt so unhappy in my job, and I didn't feel like anything I was doing was making any type of impact on others.

I had reached a point where, I felt as though I had tried every method I could think of, and it still didn't seem to make a difference. Was anyone hearing me? Was the effort I was putting in even worth it? I was beginning to think that it wasn't.

I'd been having more than my share of bad days, and I was seriously contemplating moving onto a new position because clearly, I wasn't making any difference where I currently was. Even though I was unhappy, I always made sure that I did my job effectively and didn't "phone it in" as they say.

During a 1on1 meeting with one of my employees, they told me something that really changed my view on things.

"Thank you," she said to me.

"I'm sorry, for what?" I looked up, confused, as we hadn't even been talking about anything that warranted a thank you.

"Thank you for what you do."

I didn't know what to say to that. It's very rare, and I'll say it, almost impossible to be thanked as a manager. I was so flabbergasted, I really didn't even know where to begin.

"I'm not sure I understand what you mean," I replied, unable to understand what she was getting at.

"I know you think that we don't notice how much work you do to make our lives easier, but I do. So, thank you. A few months ago, I was about to quit because I hated coming into work every day. I didn't like the people I worked with, I felt like no one was doing what they we supposed to be doing, and I was just plain miserable. You've really changed it for me. Now I look forward to work because you've built an environment that is welcoming. You're challenged me to do my best, and I've never been so motivated before. I know you think that we don't notice how much work you do to make our lives easier, but I do. So, thank you," she said this simply, but genuinely.

I will tell you, as a woman, it's a known rule to not cry at work. It makes you appear weak to some people, although that's a bunch a bunk, because that's one of the main ways most women deal with stress. I could feel the tears brimming at my eyes, but I held it back.

"Thank you. I really needed to hear that," I finally responded after making sure I had my tears under control…like a real woman!

The lesson here is that, there are so many times that you won't even really know the full impact that you make on others with the decisions and choices you make in your job. I didn't, but I was definitely wrong. So, even if you don't feel like you're seeing results, remember, that perhaps that's the way it's supposed to be, at least for now.

And remember, use your mental muscles. Live by them. You'll see your manager muscles grow, and you'll see a new response from your manager, your peers, and your employees.

10 INDEX

3 S's, 174, 182
Adversarial anchor, 52, 54, 58, 177, See Influencers
Allowed truth, 148, 149, 159, 162
ARCS, 21, 24, 27, 29, 177, 179
Assessing and managing perception, 130, 137, 176
Assumption, 131, 134
Audience, 46, 47, 53, 177
Audio communication, 43, 46
BAM philosophy, 128, 134, 137
Being transparent and credible, 146, 158, 159
Buy in process, 16, 17, 25, 28, 36, 37, 39, 52, 58, 147, 179, and 189
Change cheerleader, 38, 39, 52, 54, 58, See Influencers
COD method, 93, 95, 98, 101, 105, 106, and 112
Communication content, 45, 53, 55, 67, 177
Communication elements, 41
Communication method, 41, 42, 45, 52, 54, 56, 59, 67, 177
Complexity, 45, 46, 52, 55, 59
Continually challenging your muscles, 179, 185
Control, 79
Credibility, 150
Culture, 48, 53, 56, 59, See Audience
Demonstrating active listening, 151, 160
Demonstrating flexibility, 40, 54, 59, 67, 154, 176, 177
Developing your employees, 119, 134
Development life cycle, 123, 139
Development plan, 123, 125, 133, 136, 139, 158
Development roles, 120, 121, 122, 135,

138
Distractions, 99
Effective worker approach, 71, 72, 86
Emotion lock up process, 13, 14, 24, and 28
Feedback sandwich, 155, 162
Generation, 47, 48, 53, 56, 59, See Audience
Genuine, 140, 158, 159, 162, 163, 190
Handling difficult conversations, 67, 68, 80, 83, 154, 176
Hats, 49, 50, 51, 53, 57, 59, 154, 176, 178
Hierarchy, 48, 53, 56, 59, See Audience
Holding others accountable, 19, 27, 29, 154, 176
Immediate written communication, 45, 46
Influencers, 36, 52, 54, 58
Intent, 138, 139, 149
Looping, 97, 98
Manage through change, 176
Manager mantra, 19, 29, 68, 83, 86, 179
Managing through change, 35, 36, 53, 58
Managing your emotions, 13, 24
Managing your time wisely, 92, 106
Mental muscle, 5, 7, 30, 60, 114, 140, 182, 185
Mental muscles, 182
Multitasking spectrum, 99, 100, 107, 112
Nature of the message, 45, 46, 53, 55, 59
Nurturing, 114, 133, 139, 190
Options, 179
Organized, 75, 87, 105, 106, 113, 129, 189
Perception, 130, 133, 134, 137, 139
Perception and assumption, 131
Personality, 48, 53, 56, 59, See Audience
Planning ahead and being proactive, 103, 111
Prioritize, 94, 129, 139
Proactive approach, 103, 105, 111, 113
Providing balanced feedback, 154, 159,

161, 162
Putting all the muscles to work, 173, 183
Remaining consistent, 65, 66, 79, 85
Resolute, 60, 154, 189
Self development plan, 101, 103, 105
Self evaluation, 156, 162
Self lens view, 69, 71, 83, 86
Setting goals, 101, 108
Sharing the knowledge forward, 181, 186
SIT approach, 152, 153, 159, 160, and 162
Situation, 175
Skillsets, 176
Solution based thinking, 39, 40, and 52
Strategic, 7, 23, 29, 36, 58, 68, 154, 189
Strengths and opportunities, 154, 161, 162
Stress cycle, 127, and 136
STRONG, 5, 164, 173, 183, 187, 190
The options, 17, 23, 28, 36, 39, 58
The why, 17, 23, 28, 36, 58
Thrive or dive principle, 73, 74, and 78
Time constraints, 45, 46, 52, 55, 59
Timely feedback, 75, 76, 77, 80, 84, 86, 154
Transformative, 30, 52, 58, 67, 82, 85, 154, 189
Understanding how to balance needs, 126, 130, 136, and 139
Visual communication, 42, 46
Worst case scenario method, 179, and 180
Written communication, 44

11 REFERENCES

Hobson, A. (2004). *The Oxford Dictionary of Difficult Words.* New York: Oxford Dictionary Press .

McIntosh, C. (2013). *Cambridge Advanced Learner's Dictionary.* Cambridge : Cambridge University Press.

Wall Street Journal. (2009, April 7). How to Manage Different Generations. New York City, New York, United States of America.

ABOUT THE AUTHOR

Jorie Saldanha has over fifteen years of management and leadership experience in a variety of environments, including retail, nonprofit organizations, private sector higher education, and corporate America. Her interests include many topics as can be seen by her eclectic collection of works which includes poetry and fiction. Her other published works are *A Life Like Mine*, *A Lifetime of Passion : A Poetry Collection*, and *Summer Winds*. She lives in Hoffman Estates.

www.ingramcontent.com/pod-product-compliance
Lightning Source LLC
Chambersburg PA
CBHW051455170526
45166CB00001B/255

* 9 7 8 1 5 2 2 8 5 8 5 4 6 *